LEON PATTERSON:
A CALIFORNIA STORY

LEON PATTERSON:
A CALIFORNIA STORY

Gerald W. Haslam

with

Janice E. Haslam

DEVIL MOUNTAIN BOOKS
P.O. BOX 4115
WALNUT CREEK, CALIFORNIA 94596

Gerald W. Haslam with Janice E. Haslam

LEON PATTERSON: A CALIFORNIA STORY

©2014 by Gerald W. Haslam

DEVIL MOUNTAIN BOOKS, P.O. BOX 4115, WALNUT CREEK, CA 94596.

All rights reserved. No part of this work may be reproduced or used in any form or by any means—graphic, electronic, or mechanical, including photocopying, recording, taping, or information and retrieval systems—without written permission from the publisher. Manufactured in the United States of America.

Editorial Assistant: Barbara M. Sturges

Cover: David R. Johnson
  The cover photo as well as those following page 68 are provided courtesy of the Patterson family

Typesetter: Carol Yacorzynski

Typestyle: Palatino

Library of Congress Cataloging-in-Publication Data

Haslam, Gerald W.
   Leon Patterson: a California story / by Gerald W. Haslam with Janice E. Haslam.
       pages cm
   Includes bibliographical references and index.
       ISBN 978-0-915685-26-4 (print) --ISBN 978-0-915685-27-1 (ebook)
   1. Patterson, Leon, 1933-1954. 2. Shot-putters--United States--Biography. 3. Track and field athletes--United States--Biography. 4. Athletes--California--Biography. I. Haslam, Janice E., 1940- II. Title.
   GV1094.P38H37 2014
   796.42092--dc23

   [B]
                                                    2014000868

To our mothers, who read to us

ONE

In 1952, an epic battle in high school athletic history was fought by two competitors while they were more than a thousand miles apart. Bill Nieder of Lawrence High School in Kansas, and Leon Patterson of Taft Union High School in California, then the two greatest prep shot putters of all time, contended to be the first high school boy to break the 60-foot barrier with a 12-pound shot in official competition. The existing national record both young men sought to break was 59 feet 10 inches set three years earlier by Texan Darrow Hooper.

Sports writers in Kansas and California followed the athletes' progress, as did readers of *Track & Field News*, the sport's definitive journal. On April 9, 1952, the explosive Patterson won the contest when he burst across the dirt ring at Bakersfield's Griffith Stadium and sent the 12-pound metal ball 60 feet ¼ inch. A little over a month later, on May 10th, at the more celebrated West Coast Relays in Fresno, the Taft athlete proved his new record was no fluke when he tossed the shot 60 feet 6½ inches.

By no means did Nieder concede. On May 16th, he surpassed the Californian's new national record when he thrust the metal ball 60 feet 9¼ inches at the Kansas State Championship meet. Patterson then answered in his final high school competition, the California State Championships on May 24th in the Los Angeles Coliseum. After his initial effort failed to reach 60 feet, the Taft Wildcat's second throw traveled 60 feet 1½ inches. His third effort, with all 5,384 spectators likely riveted on him thanks to announcer Dick Nash alerting them to the situation, Patterson burst across the ring and as *Los Angeles Times* sportswriter John de la Vega reported the next day: "Blond Leon Patterson, certainly one of the gutsiest athletes ever, surged back to claim the title of the greatest high school shot putter of all time yesterday with a national interscholastic record heave of 60 feet 9⅞ inches."

Those two remarkable young men — Nieder and Patterson — were similar in that both were also blue-chip football players: Bill a center/linebacker, Leon a fullback/tackle. Ironically, neither would experience a fulfilling collegiate gridiron career due to injury or illness. Both were clean-cut, good-looking young men. Of course, they differed in many ways, too, since Nieder, who would later compete for the University of Kansas, stood 6 feet 3 inches and weighed 225 pounds by his senior year in high school, and was notably strong yet still quick. Moreover, he would grow to 6 feet 4 inches and over 240 pounds. and become not only the first collegian to top 60 feet with a 16-pound shot, but twice set world records in the event, finishing with a best of 65 feet 10 inches. He would, in addition, be a two-time national champion, and — even more impressive — a two-time Olympic medalist, gaining silver in 1954, gold in 1960.

Patterson, on the other hand, would later compete for the University of Southern California, and he seemed to be a runt among shot put behemoths at only 5 feet 11 inches and 185 pounds in high school. Nevertheless, a glance at his powerful yet trim physique revealed the source of his explosiveness: legs that produced exceptional speed and matched a preternaturally strong upper body, the product not of weight training but of a childhood characterized by hard, manual labor. As Earl Gustkey wrote in a *Los Angeles Times* article nearly 40 years later, by the time he was 14, Patterson "had the body of a powerfully built man."

During the spring of 1952 people in Taft anxiously followed Nieder's progress, while Lawrence's populace kept an eye on Patterson's accomplishments. Eventually that season, reported *Lawrence Journal-World* columnist Bill Mayer, Patterson became "a sort of villain" in Lawrence, a distant threat to the hometown favorite and, perhaps worst of all, a Californian. In fact, the tan, blond Leon Patterson did appear to be the apotheosis of the California dream, yet he was actually the product of the gritty part of the Golden State's reality: poverty, toil, deprivation. He came of age far from Hollywood, far from the state's stereotypes, in a dry corner of its heartland.

Patterson's family had migrated west from Arkansas and, like John Steinbeck's Joad family in *The Grapes of Wrath*, searched desperately for opportunities during the late 1930s and early 1940s. Leon and his older brothers, George and Calvin, grew up working as migrant farm laborers, all doing men's work as kids. "Mom and Dad followed crop harvests," explained oldest brother, George. "They were basically field hands until we got to Taft. We all were." Leon, like his two older brothers, had helped support their impecunious family by doing arduous, physical farm labor starting when he was only six years old.

The boy eventually worked and dwelled in parts of California that weren't very golden at all, yet his own potential seemed bright indeed. But there was another, far greater complication during that halcyon season of 1952, one that few knew about: Patterson turned out to be a hero, eventually recognized even in Lawrence, Kansas, once folks there learned that during his season of remarkable competition with Bill Nieder, Leon had been terminally ill with Bright's disease — a then-incurable kidney condition now called nephritis — and he had known it.

So had a dark-haired girl with horn-rimmed glasses who attended all but the most distant of Leon's meets, who helped him practice, who tutored him academically, and — most important of all — who loved him. That girl, Dixie Joanne Kenney, would stand by him no matter what the cost — and the cost would become considerable — yet she remained his rock. Together they not only won athletic competitions, but they left an indelible memory of young love's resilience.

Two

Orel Leon Patterson was born on August 21, 1933, near tiny Oark, Arkansas, on a family farm homesteaded by his great-grandfather. Home births were the norm then in rural Arkansas, where the Patterson family was rooted, and "Leon" was delivered by an aunt, who discovered that the baby's umbilical cord was wrapped around his neck. He was blue when she "got it off and cut the cord and shook life into him." Leon weighed a robust 10 pounds his aunt estimated.

The Ozark foothills were the setting of the Pattersons' home, and that region's economy was depressed even before the Great Depression. So was Leon's father, Marvin Patterson. By the time of the boy's birth, Marvin was struggling to provide for his wife, Lillie, and their older sons, George and Calvin, in a region noted for its peach production. There had been virtually no rain in 1934, then again in 1936, and plummeting prices for agricultural products generally throughout the decade led to a pervasive sense of helplessness among farmers in Arkansas, including Marvin.

Although living to the east of the wheat belt that became infamous as the "Dust Bowl," the Pattersons suffered some of the same desperation that motivated farmers in that desiccated district. The family's men tried to hang on by logging, felling trees which they finished as best they could, then sold as lumber in Clarksville or as firewood in Oark. There were many desperate, free-lance loggers in the woods then, so despite their best efforts the Pattersons could barely raise enough cash to pay for food. Pulling up stakes and seeking better opportunities in the Far West increasingly seemed the most promising course to them as to so many others. One migrant lyrically recalled, *"The Arkies and Okies in nineteen thirty-six/Cranked up their flivvers and came west Sixty-six..."*

During that period, eight out of ten Arkansas residents were said to rely upon some form of agriculture for their primary income. Cotton had long been king in the state, but cotton requires considerable water to grow. It also requires fair compensation for farmers, but "Plummeting cotton prices battered the state's economy in the 1920s," explained historian Ben Johnson, "helping to give rise to the notion that Arkansans did not notice the Depression because they were already poor." But in fact they did notice, and they were also hearing that cotton — a familiar crop — was becoming increasingly important in California's agriculture. That was true, but the sunshine-every-day, jobs-for-everyone stories that went with it were not. Still, many residents of Arkansas were tempted to seek familiar work on the unfamiliar West Coast.

Tenant farmers in particular suffered, but at least the Pattersons were free-holders. Nonetheless, in the Southern pattern, large numbers of tenants of various kinds — share renters, cash renters, etc. — worked the land in Arkansas. Ownership was concentrating in fewer and fewer hands, which made it psychologically more difficult for Marvin Patterson to let go of ownership, an act that would change his status from landowner to landless laborer, a great psychological loss. But starvation can be a persuasive force, and wages for small farmers like him and farm laborers alike were plunging. By the dawn of the 1930s, for instance, laborers in Arkansas averaged only $1.65 a day, about half the non-Southern norm. For many owners of small spreads, such as the Pattersons, reality meant no wages at all. By 1933, according to another historian, John L. Ferguson, unemployment in Arkansas — a state with scant industrial base — reached 37 percent, and taxes were delinquent on one-third of the state's rural land (including the Pattersons' farm). More than half of Arkansas's thin cadre of manufacturers had closed, while bank deposits in the state fell to less than half what they had been in 1929. One result was that in 1933 Arkansas became the only state to default on its bond payments.

At the lowest point of the Depression, according to yet another historian, Ken Bridges, one out of every four Arkansas families received Red Cross food aid. It seemed increasingly to be the time to get out and seek work elsewhere, so the state's population began a steep decline that lasted into the 1960s, causing it to lose three of its seven seats in the U.S. House of Representatives. "We wasn't 'Dusted out,'" reported Arkansas expatriate John Hillis, "we was 'Depressioned out.'" Another migrant, Frederick Soule, sang this ditty to Tom Collins in 1937:

Seven cent cotton and forty cent meat
How in the Hell can a poor man eat?
Poor, gettin' poorer all around here,
Kids coming reg'lar every year.
Fatten our hogs, take 'em to town,
All you get is six cents a pound.
Very next day you have to buy it back,
Forty cents a pound in a paper sack.

Historian James Gregory noted, "At any given point during the 1930s, somewhere between a fifth and a third of the Southwest's population suffered the effects of unemployment and severe poverty." Moving west during hard times had become a well-established American pattern by the 20th century; in the 1920s, migration from what some called the "Western South" brought approximately 250,000 new residents to California. The vast region of departure, which included the Dust Bowl, was much larger: Texas, Oklahoma, Arkansas, Missouri, Louisiana, and southern Kansas, plus the edges of several other states.

The larger picture during the desperate 1930s revealed that folks from all corners of the southwest, folks of all colors and of many backgrounds, relocated in California during that decade, and as a result many were present when World War II and its aftermath heated up the Golden State's economy, and even more migrated to the West Coast after the war. Their presence, in turn, changed and enriched the state's culture. A popular country song of the 1940s, "Dear Okie," written by Rudy Sooter and Doy O'Dell and originally performed by O'Dell, began, *"Dear Okie/ if you see Arkie/ tell him Tex's got a job for him/ out in Cali-forn-y/ pickin' up prunes,/ squeezin' oil out of olives"...* Hank Thompson later made it a major hit.

Many "Arkies" were indeed pulled west by the promise of jobs while others were pushed there by desperate conditions at home; still others — like the Pattersons — were both pushed and pulled. "As Depression came," recalled Marvin and Lillie's oldest son, George, "everyone wanted to go to California. There was a lot of promise there, everyone believed, for a better life." Moreover, the Golden State's many years of self-promotion, along with its new, plentiful cotton harvests, pulled Okies, Arkies, and Texies west, among them the Pattersons. Social historian Keith Windschuttle offered numbers: In the 1940s "about 630,000 [Southwesterners] went to the West Coast." And, as Windschuttle further points out, most weren't pickin' prunes or squeezin' oil out of olives, since they "came from cities and towns," not farms; many ended up doing industrial work and settling in various communities of greater Los Angeles. Between 1935 and 1938, according to William H. Mullins, 38 percent of Southwestern migrants settled in that urban area.

A few members of the extended Patterson family had already pulled up stakes and journeyed West before Marvin, Lillie, and their family did because, beyond its immediate allure, the West had for several generations been the direction of hope and expansion for middle Americans. "Our family left Clarksville in '37," recalled George Patterson, adding that the journey to the Golden State "took a few years...Mom and Dad would follow crop harvests along the way... So did Calvin and me." Many years later, Leon Patterson's widow, Dixie Nezat, told journalist Earl Gustkey that her husband had revealed to her that "his earliest memories were of climbing up and down ladders in Mendocino County peach orchards with a 60-pound bag hanging from his neck." Leon had been six years old when he began performing farm labor. At seven he was chopping (weeding with a hoe) cotton under glaring San Joaquin Valley sun. He later picked cotton in those same fields, his pay going to his parents, who too often drank it up.

Along their route to California, the Patterson family started on Route 66, camping where they could. George recalled a stay next to the Mojave River and another next to Camp Roberts just off Highway 101. They picked potatoes, peaches, grapes, apples. and cotton along the way. He also said the family had spent a year or so in the Phoenix area, but he didn't recall what work was done there by his parents, who had only grade-school educations. Marvin Patterson's "goal was to get to Fresno for the crop-picking jobs. Steady money, he believed. We got to Fresno and nothing was what he felt it would be, and he quickly wound up working in the oil fields" near Taft, which turned out to be a lucky break for the entire family. It was dependable employment at last, and it required no more migration.

Taft is located on the southwestern edge of California's Great Central Valley, an ancient seabed that occupies much of the center of the state. It is talked about (and presumably thought about) even by many local residents as two valleys: the Sacramento to the north, the San Joaquin to the south. Notwithstanding, it is actually a single unified trough surrounded by uplifted mountains — including the Sierra Nevada to the east, the Diablo Range to the west, the Tehachapis to the south, the Siskiyous to the north.

This vast furrow — the Great Central Valley — is the state's geomorphic core, encompassing approximately 15 million acres, about the size of England or Egypt. It is also one of California's economic engines, arguably the most productive agricultural arena in the history of the world, producing over 300 crops annually, and that is reportedly about 25 percent of all food consumed nationally. As a result, agribusiness dominates the Great Valley, for it is the sphere of agribusiness: jumbo farms and technologies of scale rather than yeomen in overalls. Beyond that, it is also one of America's richest sources of petroleum, with greater output than some OPEC nations; much of its oil is produced near Taft where the Great Central Valley pinches closed at its southwestern corner.

Terrain becomes sloping and hilly there, looking most of the year like the tan, muscular shoulders of resting cougars. In spring, those hills can briefly be lovely: "The soft colors of dry grass, sagebrush, other desert plants," recalled native daughter Dr. Hazel Hitson Weidman, "and lovely purple hues on the hills in the evenings, have influenced my color preferences throughout life." During late summer and fall, however, those same hills, shimmering in heat waves, usually appear to be cauterized and none too inviting.

In recorded history, those hills loomed above a great wetland, including to the north the largest freshwater pond west of the Great Lakes — Tulare Lake — plus the smaller Kern Lake and Buena Vista Lake to the east, all connected by sloughs and marshes. They puddled within that Tulare Lake Basin — a vast wetland with Sierran snowmelt blocked by the alluvial fans of the Kings River so that it had no natural outlet to the sea. In general, the farther south one travels in the Great Valley, the lower the annual precipitation: The section around Taft receives only about four inches to six inches of rainfall per annum, yet drainage from the distant mountains flooded the region every spring, then puddled, entrapped by the aforementioned alluvial fans — thus the wetlands. Before their drainage sources were dammed or redirected, those three lakes, like giant vernal pools, shrank as summer dried the soil. In a not uncommon California irony, their beds are now dry due to diversion of feeder streams, so are irrigated with imported water in order to grow crops there.

Where wetland bordered desert, mallards and jack rabbits shared the margin, as did tule elk and pronghorns, wolves and grizzlies. And birds so numerous that they might on occasion in flight obscure the sun, their numbers uncountable. Only the hills remain today, those and the lakebeds, since those marshes and sloughs have long since been drained, their sources of water dammed and rechanneled for systematic irrigation, so that the landscape is now called by some the "Westside Desert."

The city of Taft is situated on those dry foothills off the main line, some 40 miles southwest of Bakersfield, the seat of Kern County. Then as now Bakersfield was bisected by the historic north-south route of urban development, Highway 99, linking it to Los Angeles, to Sacramento…to the world, it seemed. The newer Interstate 5, a major north-south route west of Highway 99, now passes much closer to the Taft area than any major road has since the 18th-century Spanish cart trail, *El Camino Viejo*, did; yet it is not within sight of the town. "Eye-5," as it is called, is something of a speedway that doesn't invite touring. As a result, while prosperous, Taft and the entire Westside remain out of the way, protected by a comforting sense of detachment.

Deep beneath those southwestern hills and dry lakebeds are enormous deposits of petroleum, while above them, and supported by income from oil and related activities, are a series of small communities. They are technically part of the Great Valley's margin, but not necessarily of it: the largest is Taft, along with Maricopa, Tupman, Dustin Acres, McKittrick, Valley Acres, Ford City, Derby Acres, and Fellows. Most arose long ago when it was not practical for workers to commute to jobs, so they had to live near their oilfield work. To city slickers passing through them, the towns might appear sere and barren, but to migrants exhausted from a multi-year journey from Arkansas, they looked downright comforting.

George Patterson recalled, "We were just one family out of thousands struggling to make it up to middle class. Mom and Dad were basically field hands until we got to Taft. We all were. We lived a nomadic life, followed crop harvests. When we got to Taft, Dad had steady work for the first time in his life." The youngest son, whose given name was "Orel Leon," was already being called simply "Leon" by most. He also had a steady school for the first time in his life.

Three

The community of Taft remains the heart of the Westside, and it is oil country plain and simple. The Patterson clan found itself in a unique region, a complex of small, desiccated communities unlike any they had ever known. Long before Euro-American settlement, local native tribes employed tar-like petroleum that seeped to the surface thereabouts for many tasks. So did early Euro-American trappers and settlers. The petroleum industry there started early when, just south of Taft near present-day Maricopa, local crude oil was used as flux by white settlers in the melting of asphaltum, solid petroleum, which was quarried nearby. Because of the high daytime temperatures much of the year, as well as the impossibility of cleaning clothes, pioneer oilman Hugh Blodget recalled, "The miners worked stark naked covered with liquid asphaltum." At the end of each work day, the laborers — their bodies glistening ebony statues — scraped and scrubbed themselves as clean as possible.

Taft grew as a community in an area widely known as the Midway-Sunset oilfield, California's largest petroleum region, and the third-largest nationally. It is not quite a Great Valley town, reported native son William Rintoul, a noted oil journalist: "Taft was not so much related to areas in the farming country as it was to other oil towns like Burkburnett or Spindletop [in Texas]." He added, "It was like the roots went back to the Southwest or South." Taft's location originally offered little or no groundwater in dry years, yet sat next to seasonal Buena Vista Lake and other entrapped wetlands (or lands moist during rainy years), as well as over the vast petroleum reservoirs of the Buena Vista and Elk Hills oilfields; the latter is the largest natural-gas producing region in California and was once the nation's Naval Petroleum Reserve.

Described early in the last century as perhaps the liveliest town in the state, Taft began as a boom town, a frontier settlement in whose streets movie fans might expect Spencer Tracy and Clark Gable to brawl. Beer was for a time actually cheaper than drinking water, which had to be imported there. During its early years the entire Westside was populated largely by young white men given to male diversions — possibly not sex, drugs and rock `n' roll, but beer, brawls and bordellos certainly livened life there. Perhaps as a result of such history and the community's relative isolation, its residents have long been noted for their independence.

The surrounding Midway-Sunset oilfield has produced roughly three billion barrels of crude oil, much of it, like that asphaltum long ago quarried, so dense that an enhanced steam-recovery system has been used to liquefy it since the 1960s. Giant oil corporations such as Chevron, Shell, Exxon, Mobile, Gulf, Texaco, and Arco dominate production, but smaller companies have also found niches there. This in turn has led to an abundance of jobs, skilled and unskilled, in the oil patch.

Marvin Patterson was one of the lucky migrants indeed who escaped the seemingly endless peonage of migratory agricultural labor when he landed that oilfield job near Taft. The Patterson family settled in Derby Acres, one of the many small communities that developed locally, all closely linked with the social history of the oil industry, for oil companies owned not only much of the surrounding land but a good chunk of the communities as well. Taft and the immediate area have, as a result, had a long history of absentee ownership; thus some locals have had a brooding sense of distant, often faceless big shots controlling their destiny.

Nonwhites have been even more absent than owners, for until the relatively recent past, oilfield jobs in Central California were considered to be white men's work, period. Historian Michael Eissinger reported, "Oil companies only hired whites to work their oilfields, thereby creating communities with few women, and no minorities." Moreover, many of those who labored on the hot, treeless hills around Taft had drifted there from oil areas in the South and Southwest. It was asserted during the lily-white past, when blacks and other minorities were denied jobs in Kern County's oil fields, that "coloreds" didn't even want jobs there; they weren't capable of performing them. Only white men possessed the qualities necessary for such demanding labor — a comforting, racist assumption. So Taft, like the oil fields, grew up essentially all white, and by the 1920s the Ku Klux Klan was reported to be well established there. Certainly the Klan was established in nearby Bakersfield, the county seat. Eissinger asserted, "No place in California is more Southern than Kern County, including long-standing traditions of Jim Crow and other racist manifestations of Southern culture."

Rintoul further observed about his hometown, "There were such things as Taft's famous policy of not allowing blacks to stay overnight. Well, this came up from the South. It was not, incidentally, something that people like myself or my friends were proud of." Used to segregation in Arkansas, the Patterson family paid little attention to racial matters except when, as agricultural migrants, they found themselves working alongside nonwhites.

During the early days of the oil industry, also, many companies built "camps" — small, semi-autonomous communities — in the Westside oilfields for employees and their families. Some of those settlements were complete within themselves. Wenda Dawn, for example, recalled that Standard Oil's Tupman Camp "became a social center for the Elk Hills field. It was fully equipped with offices, cookhouse, one-room schoolhouse, cottages, large barrack buildings, and an attractive recreation hall with a rare patch of green lawn." Some camps — Standard Camp and General Petroleum Camp, for instance — even boasted swimming pools, no small luxury in those days. Dr. Weidman, who grew up on the General Petroleum Company lease, said the company had a pool on Hill 25 "that we sometimes used. It was filled with foul smelling sulfur water, but once we were used to it, the swimming was great."

Predictably, a certain rivalry arose between kids in the various camps, and Weidman recalled, "The road out of our G.P. lease area ran parallel to the fence separating it from the larger Standard Oil lease to the left. There we had stone-throwing wars with the Standard lease kids and climbed this fence to sneak into the Standard Oil swimming pool after it closed because we could not use it during the day unless we were guests of Standard Oil families."

Until irrigation systems brought water to the area, lawns were rare indeed, and Rintoul remembered playing golf on dirt fairways, saying, "You could get one heck of a bounce from a high drive." Also, few kids — no matter how poor — went barefooted because, as Dr. Richard "Dick" Henning explained, "In the summer, temperatures reached 110 degrees on most days and the oil-based pavement was blistering hot; as well there were goat-head stickers everywhere. Taking a shortcut across a field meant you would be pulling hundreds of thorns off the bottom of your shoes."

Irrigation systems increasingly have made agribusiness possible adjacent to the Westside oil fields, so seasonal farm labor such as originally attracted the Pattersons and so many others was (and is) required nearby. Jobs in the oil patch were dreamed of by many migrants, because they offered not only steady employment, but also paid well. George Patterson remembered, "When we got to Taft, Dad had steady work for the first time in his life." Marvin, like most, started at the bottom, as a "roustabout," a general helper. He then "became a well-puller and a general oilfield contractor," explained George, adding, "But his drinking held him back all his life."

Today, Taft is neat, clean and somewhat desiccated, as well as moderately prosperous, just as it was when the Pattersons arrived nearly 70 years ago. That Arkansan family was part of a multi-staged migration west from the Southwest that had been made both famous and infamous by John Steinbeck's novel *The Grapes of Wrath*. By the early 1940s, nearby Bakersfield was being called "the fourth-largest city in Oklahoma," and some local residents were outraged that Steinbeck had "demonized" — or exposed truths about — agribusiness in the Great Valley.

Ironically, the Patterson family had, unbeknownst to it, relocated close to the epicenter of the state's anti-migrant movement, which then drew strong support from the oil industry. In nearby Bakersfield, a Committee of 60 had been formed in 1938 to remove "a peril to every working man and woman...in the migrant labor and relief problem of Kern County." That group morphed into the statewide, anti-migrant California Citizen's Association (CCA) headed by Kern County luminaries such as newspaper publisher Alfred Harrell, and businessmen Arthur S. Crites and Thomas McManus. The latter famously proclaimed that "no greater invasion by the destitute has ever been recorded in the history of mankind." That so-called "invasion" didn't stop local growers from employing many of the "invaders" as field laborers at subminimal wages.

Due largely to an organized and notably dishonest campaign against migrants, the Great Valley by the late 1930s and the 1940s was no longer an especially welcoming place for Okies, Arkies and Texies, .except when growers needed them for cheap labor. As historian Walter Stein further reported, "The dominant position of oil companies among CCA's backers had political overtones," principally an effort to discredit President Franklin Roosevelt's New Deal policies, such as funding Farm Security Administration camps to house migrants.

By the time the Pattersons arrived, nearly a decade of anti-migrant propaganda had defamed Southwesterners in Kern County, as well as virtually anyone else who challenged the status quo, although those same migrants were essential to the region's economic well-being. Fortunately, nearly a half-decade of interaction had taught most folks how to get along, and history has exposed the cover of anti-migrant bigotry, exposing perpetrators such as the CCA and its often cowardly allies. That is one bit of the region's hidden history, now mostly forgotten and largely ignored by contemporary residents, who seem to assume that things have pretty much always been as they are. Migrants such as the Pattersons know better.

Four

Six-and-a-half miles northwest of Taft on Highway 33, Derby Acres was founded in the 1930s as a residential area for oil workers — part "Hooverville," part oilfield camp, part hope. It is located on the northern edge of the Midway-Sunset oilfield. Urban dwellers in California have, of course, long had the habit of dismissing the state's rural and small town reaches; for instance, *Los Angeles Times* columnist Jim Murray described Derby Acres as "little more than an oilfield junkyard with houses attached."

With a cafe and a bar, a gas station and store, as well as friendly, hard-working folks, it is described more generously by Westside historian Pete Gianopulos as "a typical area with housing for oil workers. It is not a bad location." Building codes were loose in the 1940s, land was cheap, and jobs were nearby. That's why Marvin and Lillie Patterson settled there in the 1940s shortly after Marvin found steady oilfield work. Said George Patterson, "I think Leon was 10 or 12 when we got to Taft. Dad and I built that house in Derby Acres." The youngest brother enrolled in a one-room school and, for the first time in his life, enjoyed a settled, if not entirely stable, situation; he could at least stay in the same class for an entire academic year and be a kid.

Previously, Leon had been one of those barefooted migrant youngsters who attended class for a month or two, then moved on, one of those shoeless youngsters whose handkerchiefs were snot-stiff rags, whose lunches — if any — were bread smeared with lard. Students from settled families at first wondered where boys like him came from and how they got there. Few wondered where they were going, but that's the question they should have asked.

Unfortunately, once Marvin Patterson found steady work near Taft, the family was never quite able to take a firm step into the middle class. In large measure, Marvin and Lillie simply didn't know how; their backgrounds hadn't prepared them for upward socio-economic mobility in post-World War II California, and Marvin was more apt to spend any spare money than to save or invest it. As a result, most of Leon's classmates thought of him as poor, although more than a few of them were the products of families with similar incomes.

Both of Leon's parents were drinkers, but the mother seemed to her future daughter-in-law, Dixie Kenney, to be much intimidated by her husband. Lillie was meek in his presence, and she also clearly loved her sons. Dixie later revealed that Leon had been especially close to his mother, and that he had expressed despair over his parents' drinking, particularly over his father's occasional drunken violence. An unimpressive man, Marvin seemed to be reasonable and not unpleasant when sober, but alcohol unleashed his demons; he grew domineering when drunk. Lillie drank with her husband, her sons believed, only because Marvin insisted on it. When free of him, she was an affectionate and considerate mother, something her husband seemed at times to jealously resent. Leon, her baby, remained especially close to her, and both were abused by the hot-tempered father.

Marvin and Lillie Patterson had been deeply stamped by their rural Arkansas experiences; they had, for example, rarely if ever used the services of doctors. Folk remedies — and poor recovery rates — were common in their experiences, so when their youngest son, then about 12, began to complain of trouble swallowing and his face was flushed with fever, he was put to bed with a kerosene-soaked rag tied around his throat. Although they could by then have afforded to visit a physician, they "didn't believe in doctors." Hot teas with some honey were administered, too. Leon was sick for a long while, but gradually improved. Since his parents hadn't taken him to a physician, they never knew for certain what had ailed him, but later it was speculated that his youthful energy had allowed him to survive a streptococcus infection. That apparent bout with this infection would, however, later have terrible consequences.

By the time he battled that infection, the boy was nearly a young man. Dixie, his widow, reported, "He was physically mature at 12 or 13, his body solid with muscles honed by years of hard work." At Derby Acres for almost the first time in his life he had been able to just horse around, chase up some mischief, indulge in ball games, and he seemed to be a natural athlete. In that blue-collar social environment, many men played at tests of strength, and young Leon held his own even with more mature competitors. Among his peers, everyone liked to choose him on a team because he was always among the swiftest when boys raced in P.E. class, and by far the strongest when push-ups or pull-ups were required. Dixie, who met him when she was an eighth-grader and he was a ninth-grader, remembered too that, moreover, "he felt it important to always be a good sport on the field."

Leon also told his future wife that, as a youngster, he had worked at part-time jobs — delivery boy, yard cleaner, handyman, etc. — during the school year in order to have spending money, but his parents often took his pay to buy beer. He had once hidden part of his wages in a light fixture, but his father had found it and spent it on drink. Leon had been raised in an atmosphere of pragmatic amorality: If his parents drank up the grocery money, he might have to steal bread or lunch meat or milk, and he'd done so without apparent guilt. His future wife recalled, "I once caught him slipping a couple of steaks into his coat, and I made him put them back. The way he was raised, if you didn't have the money you just took it." As a result of that experience and others, she developed some doubt about him. When they had been dating for a short time, for instance, Leon gave her "a necklace, bracelet, earring set in a green stone. It looked expensive." Many years later she admitted, "I don't know to this day if he bought it or stole it. I told him he didn't have to buy me things." In order not to put financial pressure on him, Dixie also told Leon that her favorite corsage for proms was "a single gardenia because I knew that was the cheapest corsage, so he always gave me gardenias. Sometimes he got me two instead of one. I told him they were beautiful but I only needed one."

Marvin, Lillie, and their boys settled into their small house in Derby Acres, where most of their neighbors were also from the South or Southwest; the comfortable community had an ambiance that might have been in Arkansas. Neighborliness prevailed in the other oilfield settlements, too; Dr. Weidman, growing up in the G. P. camp, remembered her family sharing a Mission fig tree with a next-door neighbor. "The tree actually belonged to the neighbor, but it was huge and half of it hung over our yard. The agreement was that anything on our side of the fence belonged to us."

Many local neighborhoods retained that comfortable ambiance. Perhaps as a result of the earlier ingress of Southwesterners of various colors, the agriculturally rich San Joaquin Valley seemed by the late 1940s and the 1950s to be producing an unexpected bonanza: world-class athletes. Tulare's Bob Mathias, whose parents had been early transplants from Oklahoma, and Kingsburg's Rafer Johnson, with Texas roots, both won Olympic decathlon gold medals. Sim Iness, another Tulare athlete with Oklahoma roots, won the Olympic discus title in 1952. Memorable others would include such standouts as Rafer's younger brother Jimmy, who earned a spot in the NFL Hall of Fame; Frank Gifford, from Bakersfield High School, another NFL Hall of Fame inductee; Fresno's Les Richter, an all-pro linebacker; Eddie LeBaron, an all-pro quarterback from Oakdale. Lon Spurrier and Leamon King, both Delano High School graduates, held world records in the 880-yard run and 100-meter dash, respectively. Future sub-four-minute miler Bob Seamon broke the national scholastic record while running for Reedly High School. Just to the west in Lemoore, Tommie Smith had begun the path that would lead him to 200-meter world records and Olympic gold. Madera native Lee Evans would set a world record for 400 meters and win the 1968 Olympic gold medal. All-Star pitcher Mike Garcia grew up in Orosi. Another All-Star chucker, Tom Seaver, started his pitching career in Fresno's Little League. Indianapolis-500 legend Billy Vukovich was also from Fresno. And on and on. It was an extraordinary time for sports in that demanding region.

Young Leon Patterson, who would soon qualify for that list of standouts, settled in at Olig School near McKittrick. Migrant children were often behind their classmates in academics, and they were also frequently placed in lower grades so that basic skills might be strengthened. That, in turn, led to the stereotype of migrant youngsters as being not only dumber but also older, larger, tougher and perhaps more sexually active than native Californians. Leon, as it turned out, was one of those with deficient basic academic skills, which he worked hard to correct after his family finally settled in.

He was especially fortunate that his parents resided in the Taft Union High School District, because oil revenues provided a strong tax base and allowed teachers there to earn high salaries but also to be held to high standards. As Dr. Dick Henning, who progressed from an oilfield kid to a college dean, pointed out, "The greatest equalizer the world has ever known is public education," and Dr. Weidman added, "We were fortunate, indeed, to go to high school in an oil-rich district that offered every advantage — particularly the caliber of teaching staff."

Leon Patterson may have been a tough athlete, but he was not impervious to the disdain some Californians expressed for migrant youngsters. Calvin Patterson recalled what was likely his little brother's introduction to organized sports. "When Leon was 12 years old, he came home from school with a frown on his face and disgust in his heart," Calvin explained. The boy had wanted to compete for Olig School in the County Schools' Championship track meet, but "the teacher had told him that he was too big and clumsy to ever take an active part in athletics." Their father, Marvin, no athlete but not one to take a slight passively either, convinced the boy that the teacher didn't know what he was talking about, that Leon was as good as anyone. "You've got to put all your effort into it, son," Calvin paraphrased his father. The next day, seventh-grader Leon ignored the teacher's comments and competed in the track meet. "I'll never forget Leon's face when he burst into the kitchen after school that day with a blue ribbon in his hand," recalled his mother. "He had taken first place in the broad jump."

From that point on, Calvin continued, Leon "took interest in basketball, football, and baseball." He played pickup games with his buddies and, living among virile oil workers, he also became known as a strong boy in a family of strong boys. George and Leon in particular were both muscular. Calvin, like his father, was lean and wiry, but stronger than he appeared. Marvin, not an athlete in a formal sense, was reputed in the family to have had a powerful, accurate throwing arm, able back in Arkansas to knock squirrels from trees with rocks he pitched.

Adolescent Leon, meanwhile, would occasionally indulge in tests of brawn against full-grown men who took pride in their own vigor, and he seemed always to hold his own. Sometimes a nickel or a dime would be bet on who could lift what; Leon seldom lost. Even seasoned oil workers considered him something of a prodigy. His parents remembered him — without any systematic strength training — hoisting his body weight, 165 pounds, over his head when he was 15.

In those years before air-conditioning became available in homes, a local wag suggested that hot weather on the Westside and thereabouts caused many kids to physically mature early, having 25-year-old bodies controlled by 13-year-old minds. Leon Patterson seemed to be one of them, shaving at 13, though thinking and behaving like a kid.

His widow, Dixie, recalled when they first met at a Fosters Freeze when she was in junior high, and he was a high school freshman. Leon hung around and flirted like the other boys, but she could tell he was shy. He later told her he had decided to marry her then. She told him, "But you didn't even know me." He had grinned and replied, "But you had great legs and chest."

Dixie, as it turned out, had also physically developed early. Raven-haired and trim, she was one of Taft Union High School's beauties, not only a top student but also — in those days before Title IX equalized opportunities for women — she was nearly as athletic as her future husband; eventually she was named Taft Union High School's outstanding female athlete. She also modeled bathing suits for a local store when she was 13. The fashion show was held at the public swimming pool, and she recalled "some guys hooting and clapping when I came out. Later a friend of mine who was in the audience said that one guy tried to get my phone number from her. I don't know if it was Leon." If it was, Leon had chosen well, although he didn't vigorously pursue her at the time.

FIVE

As a result of his accomplishments at the aforementioned county track meet, young Leon Patterson's potential as an athlete became known to at least some coaches at Taft Union High School before he enrolled there. TUHS was a secondary school with a large but thinly populated service area (Taft's population in 1950 was only 3,707), thus having a somewhat limited student population. Nevertheless, the Wildcats were noted for their willingness to compete against larger and more diverse institutions. In fact, Taft's class of 1952 seemed especially gifted athletically, with future standouts like Don Zumbro, Elvie Dalton, Charles Hanna, Gary Green, Ray Herman, and Dennis Cutland, among others, who would win glory for the school along with athletic scholarships to various colleges for themselves.

Those boys would eventually enter a somewhat different nation than their elders had grown up in because, following World War II, America continued changing, or so it seemed.

In June of 1948, President Harry S. Truman signed into law The Selective Service Act that would require registration of all men between the ages of 18 and 25, and a military draft to assure certain minimal strength for the various branches of the armed forces. That legislation would profoundly impact the lives of young, working-class males in places like Taft for decades to come.

Perhaps the biggest news in the San Joaquin Valley was that a little over a month after Truman signed the Selective Service Act, the first post-war Olympic games were held in London, England, and 17-year-old Bob Mathias from nearby Tulare High School won an unexpected gold medal in the men's decathlon. Then, in November, Democrat Truman was reelected President of the United States, much to the surprise of Republican candidate Thomas E. Dewey — and to the surprise of many voters in Kern County. "I think it was rigged," said one disgruntled oil worker. "I don't know one guy that voted for that booger."

Teens in Taft during the dynamic post-war period — some of whom had competed in high school events against Olympic champion Mathias only a few months earlier — didn't much resemble the versions of their generation that would later be aired on TV shows and in movies, since a certain hard edge from economic adversity lingered. The previous two decades had been dominated by the Great Depression, then by World War II, and memories of hardship remained fresh in the late 1940s. Nevertheless by 1948, despite hints of communism's threat providing a dark edge, a more hopeful time was dawning. Just around the corner Little Richard was ready to replace Bing Crosby, Lucille Ball would hold a comic mirror up to domestic life, and Bunny Yaeger's camera — famous for *Playboy* photo spreads — would expose more skin than even dermatologists were accustomed to seeing.

A period of opportunity and upward mobility was upon the land, especially in California which had been virtually remade economically during the war, and erstwhile Depression migrants would benefit. Leon Patterson's older brother, George, broke with family patterns and left home for a career in law enforcement, much to his parents' discomfort. Like so many young migrants, he was becoming a Californian with a Californian's sense of the possible, and his younger brothers were on the same trajectory. Calvin soon joined the military.

At Taft Union High School there remained, of course, jocks and rowdies, princesses and pushovers. A few girls might wear poodle skirts and peasant blouses, but others sported pedal pushers or scandalous short-shorts. Many adults in the Taft area and thereabouts in those days thought teenaged boys had adopted what was virtually a uniform: blue jeans (preferably Levis), sport shirts or white T-shirts, loafers or boots. Despite the nearly constant sun, headgear — other than cowboy hats — was rarely sported by males, but hair was carefully combed, perhaps duck-tailed, or buzzed into a flat-top.

Prior to ninth grade Leon Patterson had only participated in organized sports at the county track meets, but he had become something of a sandlot terror; "Choose 'Lee' or 'Pat'" — as he was then being called — was an axiom in his neighborhood. Fall of 1948, as a ninth-grader, he came out for the high school football team, and there was discussion among coaches Dean Johnson, Paul Smith, and Monty Reedy about whether he should play on the "B" class Bobcat squad — usually made up of freshmen and sophomores, with a few of the smaller upper classmen — but the coaches, along with athletic director Vern "Moon" Mullen (an ex-professional football player), finally decided that Patterson was mature enough to make a contribution to the Wildcats, as the varsity was called.

It was a practical decision since most of the "B" players were much less physically developed than Leon, so assigning him to the varsity lessened the chance he might hurt a teammate in practice. One of those players, Charlie — now Dr. Charles — Hanna, who would quarterback the varsity a few years later, chuckled when he said, "Leon's body was four or five years more developed than ours. He had no fat and we had no muscle."

It didn't take clairvoyance to recognize that here was a young man with tremendous physical potential, but one who was quiet and apparently not aggressive off the field. Coaches wondered how smart and how competitive he was. For himself, Leon was proud to have been placed on the varsity, but he was also a respectful underclassman, listening to his coaches and to varsity veterans, learning daily the skills that might one day make him a formidable gridder. He played selectively but well that first football season as backup to varsity fullback Bruce Freeman, and he also occasionally subbed for tackle Glenn "Tex" James. Leon learned a great deal about the game that year, and the coaches learned a great deal about him. He didn't, however, seem to realize how exceptional it was for a freshman to even suit up with the varsity Wildcats, let alone to earn playing time. He also made friends easily with his fellow players, impressing them with his attitude as well as his physical ability, especially his speed.

Throughout that school year, Leon also got to know Taft's equipment manager, Tom O' Brien, who would become his future weight-event coach in track as well as a particular friend. Athletics trainer Hillman "Shug" Shugart would become another buddy of the boy who seemed to crave male role models.

The Wildcats won three games and lost five that season, playing in the large schools' South Yosemite League. The thin roster meant that one or two key injuries could significantly weaken the team. Nevertheless, Taft had a well-deserved reputation for athletic excellence. Writer (and TUHS alumnus) William Rintoul suggested that the enduring reputation was earned during California's loosely regulated early days of interscholastic sports, when many physically fit young men — some in their twenties — were employed in the oil fields and, legend has it, that some of them took courses to finish secondary school and also competed on Wildcat teams. Taft was seen as a place where tough physical work created hard-nosed athletes. One-time Bakersfield High football standout, Marvin Mosconi, reflected, "It seemed like Taft always had a bunch of big oilfield roughnecks suited up." He added, "They were rugged."

The children and grandchildren of some of those early, somewhat mature jocks went to school with Leon Patterson, and many of them did heavy work as summer replacements in the oil patch or as seasonal farm laborers. In those days before weight training became common, at least some of Taft's players had muscled up by lifting pig iron on drilling rigs or bucking hay on nearby farms.

The high school drew students from that restricted if widely scattered population due to all the surrounding oilfield camps and small communities. Leon, for instance, rode the school bus to TUHS six-plus miles from Derby Acres, meeting his buddy Elvin Urquhart, who was traveling thirty-five miles from the Belridge lease. In those innocent days, the boys stayed late on campus for athletic practices, then hitch-hiked home each afternoon or evening if they couldn't catch a ride with a teammate.

Leon was by then a handsome, muscular youngster, as well as something of a charmer. Dixie recounted talking with girls "who lived out that way [Derby Acres] and he was really liked by everybody. Most of the girls had crushes on him." She added, "The young guys on the bus would try sitting by him because they knew he wouldn't let the bigger boys pick on them."

Taft High's population then was almost exclusively white, with a few Latinos and an occasional Asian. It was rumored to be a "sundown town" that prohibited blacks from even overnight stays, let alone residence. Nevertheless, its teams held their own against institutions with larger, often multi-ethnic student populations, such as secondary schools in Bakersfield, Fresno, Visalia, Porterville, Delano, East Bakersfield, and Tulare. The San Joaquin Valley's large population of white Southwestern migrants all seemed to be called "Okies" in those days.

Promiscuous use of that term tended to subsume everyone from Missouri to Louisiana to Colorado who had migrated west during the Great Depression and thereafter. Nonwhite migrants, especially African American, were not usually included in the regional description, although they constituted a formidable group indeed. Instead, racial (and racist) terminology tended to be used in reference to them, although many of them, too, were Depression migrants from the Southwest.

Social class and exclusivity motivated many nativists; some merely sought to avoid contact with "Okies," while others actively disdained them. Reported Jeff Nickell, "The toll on migrant children was heavy. Many of them were discriminated against in the classroom and on the playground by other children and teachers alike." Nevertheless, school was one place where in the long run egalitarianism tended to rule. Also, unlike migrants to agricultural areas, the parents of those who settled in oil country often had full-time jobs, no matter how menial, and all work was respected; in fact, employment in the oilfields was much coveted. Districts with multiple secondary school campuses, such as Bakersfield or Fresno, might *de facto* separate the affluent from the poor by selecting campus locations or district boundaries, but in single-district communities like Delano or Wasco or Taft the high school could become a social blender.

Most of those schools taught lessons about tolerance despite occasional outbursts of class bigotry or racial prejudice, or of retaliatory anger. Some teachers complained about the southwestern migrants' "bad English," although trained linguists could have explained that the regional dialects spoken by most so-called "Okies," "Arkies," and "Texies" were legitimate, if often unpolished, variations of American speech. Nevertheless, many Californians harbored the self-serving illusion that Southern and Southwestern speech patterns were inherently inferior — largely because they tended to hear them spoken by uneducated people — although the same dialects were being spoken by such "inferiors" as Katharine Anne Porter, J. Frank Dobie, Robert Penn Warren, Flannery O'Conner, or even Woody Guthrie, plus a good many senators and representatives, all of whom skillfully employed versions of Southern and Southwestern dialects.

Nevertheless, the "Okie-Arkie-Texie" children's speech patterns were mocked by some peers, and "As late as 1949, the Yuba County School System classified the accent of children from Southwestern backgrounds as a 'speech defect' and targeted it for special educational programs," reported historian James Gregory. By the time Patterson was in high school, many Southwesternisms could be heard as a normal part of oilfield lingo. One of Leon's classmates, Wildcat basketball star Don Zumbro, explained, "I believe Leon had a slight twang. I never noticed, for I was from Oklahoma."

More than a few newcomers and their families, like the Pattersons, had been living on the road for a long time, so their children had not acquired a solid academic base. Leon Patterson's future wife, Dixie, said he "was a smart kid, but by the time he got to Taft High, with his parents moving from one crop-picking job to another, he'd been to 42 grammar schools. [Patterson's brother later said it was 22 grammar schools.] He was never caught up in his schooling."

Leon, of course, grew up both formidable and pleasant, so he didn't have to put up with much teasing the way some other Southwestern kids did. Everyone seemed to like him; classmate Pat Jamerson said, "He was a great guy, not full of himself, but we didn't know how poor he was." Charlie Kooken agreed, "He was a good guy — a pretty straight arrow," but "Leon was in dire straits, really poor." They also didn't know the reason he remained poor. Leon's father had a steady job, but he also had that steady habit: The boy didn't talk about his father's drinking, let alone about the occasional violent outbursts he and his brothers, as well as his mother, endured.

Another reason Leon was spared teasing was that by the late 1940s tension between social or regional groups on the Westside was diminishing; many so-called "Okies" had become economically stable, and their appearance and their behavior was little different from that of many long-time Californians. Discussing the process of socio-economic integration, Bruce Berryhill's 1976 study of former Oklahomans living in nearby Visalia showed that those with an incentive altered their behavior and their spoken usage to more closely resemble California patterns. Not only did they change, but they in turn changed the local culture; country music was becoming the region's anthem; biscuits and gravy rivaled ham and eggs in local cafes; hard-shell Pentecostal churches thrived throughout the region. The ambitions of young migrants were no longer limited to agrarian possibilities and, as Berryhill established, those who earned middle-class positions tended to have become adept in California speech patterns, just as Leon did. His parents did not.

Rumors and more than rumors had it that Leon had a few scrapes with the law, none serious, but difficulties from which his teachers and coaches extracted him. He could easily have developed in a less positive direction without three influences: first, the independence of his older brothers, George and Calvin, who had refused to be limited by his family's pattern. They tried to mentor their youngest brother from afar. Another was Leon's relationship with Dixie Kenney, who was an outstanding student and athlete, and whose straight-arrow family embraced him; the Kenneys exposed Leon to middle-class values and ambitions he had not previously experienced. Finally, the intimate relationship he would develop with coach Tom O'Brien and the O'Brien family also reinforced everything the Kenneys valued, and then some. Both families taught him by example.

Lynne O'Brien Shelton says she has "wonderful memories of Leon and my father and their special relationship." As for Leon, whom she thought of as a brother, she "always loved his rare combination of choir-boy and naughty-boy smile." Tom and Dolores's daughter also said that Leon would visit on Sunday mornings when waffles and bacon were usually served in the O'Brien household, and Dolores "would always say, 'I've made some extras,' and he'd eat." Offered leftovers to take home, though, he'd say, "I don't want to take anything." But, of course, he did take something — their love, and it would prove to be of great consequence to him.

Leon had never had much of a Christmas celebration at home, not even a decorated Christmas tree, he told Dixie. Moreover, he had also "never had a salad until I married him," his widow reported. In fact, he loved to eat and would try virtually anything. At the local hamburger stand, he loved to order a 'burger size' [chili burger], also chili dogs with an Orange Julius." He had a growing young man's appetite. He was long on hunger but short on social graces until the Kenney and O'Brien families taught him by example.

It was also no small thing for him to dedicate himself to school, since his parents did not support education beyond bare fundamentals; they simply did not understand it. Their own experiences had been too limiting. As James Gregory noted, "Many of the migrants shared a vaguely populist outlook which directed expectation towards manual occupations and away from extended schooling." The elder Pattersons were not necessarily typical, since historian Walter Stein, on the other hand, asserted that once established, migrants "doggedly sought education for their offspring. Their move to California was designed to better their conditions, and schooling for the children was part of that design." That was especially true after World War II when new opportunities developed.

Dr. John Collins, for a time track/cross-country coach (and later president) at nearby Bakersfield College, was a Missouri native and he recalled talking to the Southwestern parents of young athletes he was recruiting, and having to convince them that the agrarian skills they had grown up with wouldn't necessarily suffice for their children in mid-century California. "It took some convincing for them to allow their kids to attend college, but the community has benefited as much as those families have." Some of those were given parental permission to enroll in the community college, he recalled, but only on the condition that they also remain available to pick cotton in season.

On the football field or in the boxing ring, on the basketball court or on the baseball diamond, migrant athletes — like migrant soldiers at the same time — were noted for their grit. Historian Gregory summarized migrant toughness this way: "Tenacity was more than the key to success; there could be no dignity, manhood, or self-esteem without it." As a result, "A preoccupation with toughness...became one of the cornerstones of the Okie subculture." The migrant kids who had to fight their way out of poverty, no matter what their color, just seemed more tenacious than others. Leon Patterson certainly fit that mold. When asked if her late husband had any fist fights at Taft Union High School during that era of frequent fisticuffs, Dixie replied, "Who'd want to fight Leon? They'd have to be crazy."

Young Patterson went out for the varsity baseball team that spring and made the cut. He wasn't experienced, but his natural athleticism rendered him valuable even though he was for all practical purposes a beginner. Leon usually played first base or pitcher. "He could run, he could catch and throw, and he swung the bat pretty well. Turns out he became a pretty valuable utility player," reported teammate

Milt Stark, who himself went on to be inducted into the International Softball Congress Hall of Fame.

One afternoon following practice, according to what has now become a local legend, Patterson was walking across the track on his way to the locker room when a Wildcat discus thrower — no one remembers exactly who — tossed a platter in his direction. Patterson picked it up and tossed it back, but it went over the other thrower's head into the bleachers. A variation of this story has Leon leaping over the high jump bar at 5 feet 10 inches in his baseball uniform on his way across the field. In some fashion or another, he seems to have much impressed the track coaches because by his sophomore year, he was on their team and became a quality competitor. Says Stark, "Needless to say, he never played baseball after that freshman season."

SIX

As a sophomore at TUHS, Leon again backed up Bruce Freeman at fullback and Tex James at tackle on the varsity football team. He had entered his second year of high school in 1949 weighing nearly 170 pounds and standing 5 feet 10 inches and was among the team's quickest players. Leon was "a loper, deceptively fast," recalled teammate Don Zumbro. The squad's leaders were seniors Milt Stark, Lige Morris, and Tex James, and the Wildcats won five and lost three, claiming all home contests but dropping all away games. The big victory was 13-6 over favored Merced High School, and Leon played an important, if unexpected, role in that upset.

As teammate Stark remembered, Patterson:

...had been sent in to give Tex a breather at right tackle. A pass play was called out of the single wing formation and somehow Leon, an ineligible receiver, found his way downfield. Lige Morris, finding all of the receivers covered, spotted Leon open about 15 yards downfield

and fired him a perfect strike. Leon caught the ball and ran for another five yards or more before being tackled. He came running back to the huddle with that big grin on his face as if nothing was out of order. No flag had been thrown, so in the huddle we told Freeman to get to the sideline and tell coach Jim Duncan to send Tex in to play tackle and we would keep Leon in at fullback.

Taft scored the winning touchdown on that series of downs. Stark summed it up: "An ineligible, inexperienced offensive tackle had caught a pass and gained over 20 yards, leading to the deciding touchdown in a 13-6 win."

Dixie, who by then never missed one of Leon's games if her job didn't interfere, cheered with the rest of the crowd although she, too, probably didn't understand exactly what had happened on that play, and neither did Leon until upperclassmen later explained. Like many students at Taft Union High School, Dixie was a working-class youngster and was expected to provide her own spending money, not out of desperate need but for the lesson it taught. She was also expected to put some away in a savings account, so she tried always to have a part-time job. Leon worked part-time, too, and most of his salary went for his living expenses. He pumped gas at the station in Derby Acres his sophomore and junior years at Taft High, recalled his pal Elvin Urquhart, then worked at another service station in Taft his senior year.

Patterson had entered that second year of high school in 1949 not only as an established player on the Wildcat varsity football squad but, reported *Los Angeles Times* journalist Earl Gustkey, "The girls of Taft High held an election to determine 'the ideal composite man.'" They voted for male classmates "with the 'best smile,' 'best clothes,' 'best car,' 'best personality,' 'best eyes,' etc. The runaway winner in the 'best build' category was Leon Patterson."

Leon was not, however, "best student," although his peers considered him bright. All those years of living as a migrant hadn't allowed him to build a strong academic base.

He struggled to catch up in his schooling, "so I helped him a lot," said Dixie. One of Leon's closest buddies, Dick Henning, confirmed Dixie's role: "She was smart, and I think she helped him with his senior-year studies." His Derby Acres neighbor Sudie Walrath also helped Leon with his homework.

On a personal level, the real and unexpected high point for Leon that tenth-grade year was that he began to date Dixie Joanne Kenney. He had met her the year before at the local Fosters Freeze when she was an eighth-grader. They didn't go out together on an official date until the next year when Dixie was a high school freshman and Leon was a sophomore, but his interest in her continued after their initial meeting at Fosters Freeze. "I think he *likes* you," her friends insinuated with the tone only adolescent girls seem to master. In fact, she too suspected he might like her, because Leon was disarmingly candid; it was as though he didn't know the rules of pairing up, so he wore his heart on his sleeve. She could read his glances and smiles from afar.

All the while, with Dixie's own interest in sports, she remained well aware of him, too, but there were still surprises in store for her. "Leon and I really met because of his artistic talent," she recalled:

> We both took art from Mrs. Steineger, but in different classes. When it came to talent she could bring out the best in you. Leon created an incredible bird which hung from a line that stretched from one eye-hook to another clear across the room. Most of the other birds looked like cardinals, bluebirds, etc. Then Leon's incredible phoenix like no other I've ever seen dominated the whole room. I couldn't take my eyes off of it.

Dixie asked Mrs. Steineger which student had created the phoenix and if she could buy it. "More important," she added, "I wanted to see what kind of person created it." When it turned out to be by the jock who had been eyeing her, "We got together and, of course, he wouldn't sell it, but he did give it to me. Shortly after that he asked me out on our first date."

When 16-year-old Leon finally began dating Dixie, he borrowed his brother Calvin's car because he "didn't like to double date much, even with close buddies like Elvin," explained his future wife, "so we went out alone." Leon, who wasn't nearly as shy in private as he was in public, quickly seemed to adore Dixie.

In a handwritten, unpublished memoir, Dixie recalled that first date:

> Our first date Leon picked me up in his brother Calvin's 1941 black Ford coupe. We went to the Fox Theater and saw "The Great Caruso" starring Mario Lanza, a favorite singer of mine. In this movie he sang "Because." This became our song. Leon bought us both a coke and we shared a large popcorn. When he parked in front of our house, I decided he wasn't going to get out and open the door for me as I was accustomed to, so I turned to open the door and Leon turned me around and kissed me. He French-kissed me which really surprised me. I never kissed on the first date and had never had a French kiss. This frustrated me, but I rather liked it. I later learned he had dated a senior girl when he was a freshman and she had taught him to French kiss.

Many years later, Elvin Urquhart revealed what was likely the actual source of Leon's knowledge of kissing. "When we were in high school, Leon and I and my sister and some of her friends (two years older than us) were driving around Taft when we decided to go to the movies at the Fox Hippodrome Theater. We sat in the balcony where the girls taught us how to kiss. Leon and I loved it. We took turns watching the movie and kissing. It was wonderful and Leon and I were very happy." Then he added, "Of course, I didn't kiss my sister." Those times were by no means as innocent as that memory might suggest, but the open sexuality of the 1960s — brought on in part at least by the availability of birth-control pills — did later create the impression of comparative virtue in the 1950s.

Meantime, Leon continued to ride to school most days with his buddy Elvin, who had acquired a 1932 Pierce Arrow from an uncle who owned a car-rental business in Southern California. "I got a license so I could pick up supplies and do the banking for my folks' store" in Belridge, Elvin explained. The driver had also learned a local trick. The surrounding oil fields were criss-crossed by pipes carrying oil and gas, and Elvin "took Leon 'dripping' on the way to school. In the cold early morning, natural gas liquefied where the lines crossed ravines. We would catch the 'drips' in a felt hat, straining out the impurities. Then we used 'Peptone' to prevent it from burning the valves in the motor." More than a few cars thereabouts suffered permanent damage from using what locals called "drip" while forgetting to add Peptone. Such appropriating from the oil companies was illegal, which made it deliciously tempting for teenagers.

As he dated Dixie, Leon got to know her parents, and he became increasingly fond of them, too. The Kenneys, who sensed not only the boy's poverty but also his yearning for affection, welcomed him into their house — indeed, into their household. "Patterson, with only a marginal family life of his own," observed journalist Gustkey, "responded eagerly to the affection shown him by Dixie Kenney." Gustkey might have added, "and by her family."

Dixie's father, Maurice Patrick Kenney, was an avocational inventor who worked for the Standard Oil Company for 41 years. Mr. Kenney was not only creative, but also handy. He "could make anything out of wood or metal on his old belt lathe," wrote Dixie. He and Leon got along "very well" and, said Dixie, "I think Leon would have liked to have had a dad like him." Moreover, Dixie whose lone sibling, sister Patricia, was 10 years older than she, admitted, "My dad had always wanted a boy"; in Leon he found a boy who had long wanted a real father.

Dixie's mother, Minnie, also accepted her younger daughter's new boyfriend. "When Leon came to see me she put him to work along with me," said the future Mrs. Patterson, "but she always fed him, too." Before Leon entered her life, Dixie explained, "I rather became a tomboy. I helped my father put in a driveway, sidewalks, patio, under the clotheslines, all behind the house in cement." Unlike Leon, Dixie Kenney's early life was stable; she attended one grade school, one junior high, and one high school, all in Taft. She was a Girl Scout, then a Senior Mariner Scout, and was also the first female recipient of Block "L" at Lincoln Junior High.

Classmate Dick Henning recalled, "Dixie was attractive; she was also muscular, solid build. She definitely looked like an athlete, and she loved sports and being around athletic teams." He added, "She was an outstanding girls' field hockey player." Charlie Hanna agreed, saying, "She was pretty and built solidly." In P.E., Dixie reported, she was the only girl strong enough to lift "the big, heavy girls on my legs." She weighed 130 pounds, but looked slimmer, and she was even known to be the only girl at the high school who could lift off the floor a 212-pound anvil that sat in the equipment room of the gym. Taft Junior College at that time shared that same gymnasium with the high school and, after college guys had failed, trainers Tom O'Brien and Ralph "Dad" Freeman used to bet them that a high school girl could hoist the heavy, awkward anvil. "I lifted it with my legs without any trouble," she recalled, adding "Leon could lift it easily."

Dixie had been only 14 when she started dating Leon, who was barely 16. As a result, both would experience wide sweeps of emotion without the mitigating effects of experience. For instance, during her first year at Taft High, Dixie was chosen one of four girls to represent Taft Chamber of Commerce on a float that went to all the parades in the San Joaquin Valley. "Leon was proud of this," she explained, "but didn't like me being gone." Having long experienced what might be considered somewhat of a loveless childhood, the boy was extremely possessive of this girl he was beginning to adore.

After she had begun dating Patterson, Dixie came to understand that the life she had taken for granted was in fact a gift. "While I was learning piano, playing violin in the orchestra, and singing in six different groups, Leon was chopping and picking cotton, living outside much of the year camping. Camping to my family was recreation, to Leon a way of life." Both Leon and Dixie were learning things — each from the other — as a result of their intensifying relationship, and so was her family.

"My dad knew Leon didn't have much money, so he hired him to help dig out under our house," she recalled. "Mom wanted a room there." After having dug the space, Mr. Kenney kept the boy on to help cement the floor and walls. Dixie added, "I had the job of shoveling sand and cement into the cement mixer, adding water, mixing it and then stopping the mixer...pouring out the cement into buckets, and carrying the buckets down to Leon and Dad." Meanwhile, "Leon tried to meet me at the doorway so I wouldn't have to carry them." Doing that kind of work at home, little wonder she could lift an anvil at school.

About that same time, teammates noticed that when they drove Leon home from school, he never invited anyone in. Few suspected that the Pattersons had only an outhouse or that Leon never knew who'd be sober or who'd be drunk. Dixie also remembered that "Leon's home was always clean when I visited, and he always had on clean clothes. Lillie washed outside in an old wringer washer. We had rugs on the floor, they had a piece of linoleum in their living room." She also remembered that "The Patterson kitchen didn't have cabinets. It had a wooden counter with shelves underneath that Lillie had put material over to cover the shelves. Most of the time his mother cooked beans. Or eggs. Ham hocks and beans were for a special occasion." There were also stories about Leon having to seek food from neighbors or teammates, or even from the cafe in Derby Acres, when his parents were drinking.

Many years later, Leon Patterson, Jr., said that his mother and others had been too harsh in their assessment of his dad's parents. He referred to Marvin and Lillie as "decent hard-working people," and said that he and others of their grandchildren had "fond memories of good times" at Grandma and Grandpa's house in Derby Acres. Of course, by the time the grandkids knew them, the Pattersons had been through a lot and had aged and mellowed.

Derby Acres, like the rest of the Westside, was a natural desert that enjoyed only about four to six inches of rain most years. It was also prone to flash floods if unusual storms occurred. "One time we had a flash flood. and the Pattersons thought they were going to lose their outhouse," Dixie recalled. "The water, I guess, filled the hole and caused lots of problems. After the flood, Leon had to dig another outhouse hole and move the outhouse over it."

Leon and his brothers had also dug another pit that allowed Marvin, as well as his sons, to work under cars, which were driven or pushed over it. The trench was deep enough to allow the men to stand and examine and repair the undersides of vehicles. During the flash flood, it turned into a pond that collected some detritus from the swamped outhouse, so it too had to be filled, then replaced by another excavation.

Seven

Dixie soon figured out that Leon didn't own many clothes, but also recognized that his mother kept what he did have clean and neat. Photos from 1949 show him pretty much in the teenage boys' uniform — jeans and short-sleeved shirt — his dishwater blond hair somewhat bleached by ubiquitous Valley sunlight. He was trim-waisted with broad shoulders — lean and muscular rather than thick or bulky.

"Leon liked clothes," remembered Dixie, "but his taste was pretty awful." To illustrate, she continued, "One time he bought some shoes that looked like spats. He asked me how I liked them. I said they look swell. The Hawaiian shirt he liked was really loud, but it made him happy, so I told him he looked fantabulous; he grinned from ear to ear." She also recalled that "He loved to wear T-shirts that showed off his magnificent physique. He especially loved a fishnet shirt he had in white."

Once the young couple began going steady, Leon made it a point to begin meeting Dixie at school in the morning and carrying her books to class. The couple soon attended a Sadie Hawkins Dance in costume, she as a version of Daisy Mae, complete with ragged shorts; he as a version of Li'l Abner, complete with a rope belt. They were a striking duo indeed. But, of course, like most youthful couples they had to blend different tastes, different expectations, and different means. They attended — along with the Sadie Hawkins affair —the Christmas Ball, the Spring Prom, the Cinderella Ball, plus post-game sock hops that featured what Dixie thought of as 50s music: songs like "Come On-A My House," "Vaya Con Dios," "Because of You," "Green Door," and so on.

Jitterbug was becoming increasingly popular, but at first Dixie and Leon favored "fox trots and waltzes." Some of his buddies later said they didn't remember Leon dancing much at all, but Dixie said, "We loved to dance and could do just about any dance that came out. Over at Bakersfield he took me to a western dance floor and he taught me western-style dances." It was probably inevitable that the two gifted athletes who loved to dance would gravitate to jitterbug. "The couples would make lots of room for us when we jitterbugged. Leon liked to show off by throwing me around a lot, and I could carry him piggyback off the floor, so crowds loved it."

Dixie's musical tastes, however, had long been cultivated at home and at school, and they had originally run to "classical, ballet, opera," while he "liked country western." Growing up, she had also studied ballet and tap dancing, while the songs of Hank Williams, Lefty Frizzell, and the Maddox Brothers & Rose were more to Leon's taste; one of his favorite records, she remembered, was Eddy Arnold's "Cattle Call."

Leon had in any case picked a good place to favor those kinds of songs, since Kern County was in those years in the throes of becoming the West Coast center of country-western music, and a force nationally due to the emergence in nearby Bakersfield and thereabouts of stellar performers such as Bill Woods, Herb Henson, Billy Mize,

Jean Shepard, Ferlin Husky, Buck Owens, Tommy Collins and, eventually, of a contemporary of Leon's named Merle Haggard. Local bars, honky-tonks, and ballrooms featured many entertainers who would soon be major country-music stars. For example, future Hall of Famer Ferlin Husky and his band played at everything from high school dances to used-car-lot openings in Kern County under the name Terry Preston and the Termites.

Teenagers on the Westside often gathered at Abram's, a drive-in at Ford City, reported Elvin Urquhart, adding, "Everyone went there after Friday night games." Other teenage hangouts were the Youth Center (also called the "Rec Center"). "They had ping-pong and other activities and a coke machine. And Milo's Downtown Drugstore. It had a soda fountain." Urquhart added, "We didn't go to Bakersfield much."

Patterson that sophomore year went out for and made the varsity basketball team, although he was by no means a polished player. He could run and jump with the best, though. A team photo in his basketball uniform shows his well-developed but not exceptionally muscled, upper body; it also reveals the notable musculature of legs that might have supported a power lifter or, paradoxically, a ballet dancer. "He was not a starter but played some," recalled basketball star Don Zumbro, who added, "He would have made a great hit man!" — the name for what is now called an on-court "enforcer."

When track coach Les Voorhees learned that the husky blond would be coming out for the track team in the next spring, he at first thought of Leon as a natural sprinter-jumper. As the season approached, there were more and more discussions among Voorhees and Tom O'Brien about which events Leon might best contest. He was fast enough for the sprint relay team, and he could with no special training long jump beyond 20 feet and high jump over 5 feet 10 inches. Shown how to vault with a stiff bamboo pole, he cleared 11 feet in P.E. class, then later in competition. Also in P.E. class, Leon influenced another athlete. Teammate Jack Howard said, "I beat Leon in the mile in P.E., so I was 'the miler' from then on. No more racing Leon."

Patterson's rare combination of speed, strength and coachability convinced O'Brien that Leon was a future champion in the shot and discus, and O'Brien's interest was Leon's good luck. Tom O'Brien, who served officially as trainer and equipment manager for the high school, was in fact a student of the throws, which he coached for the Wildcats. "Coach O'Brien had the best varsity, 'B'class, and 'C' class shot putters in the Valley every year," according to rival Gary Ogilvie, who both competed for then later coached track and football at Bakersfield's Garces Memorial High School and at Tehachapi High School. "He knew more about shot put, conditioning, and discipline than anyone I ever met," recalled Ogilvie. He also remembered that, at a major meet in Santa Barbara, Parry O'Brien, the world record holder in the 16-pound shot, "came and asked some guy standing next to me where Tom O'Brien might be." He found Tom and asked him if he would watch him throw; he was having a few problems." Concludes Ogilvie, "The little old equipment man from Taft High went out to help the world record holder. Priceless."

More importantly, Tom O'Brien would also become for Leon Patterson far more than a coach; like Mr. Kenney he would become a father figure. Thomas O'Brien was a native of Ireland, who had moved to Taft as an eight-year-old in 1921. He matured in the community and served it not only as mentor and friend to young athletes, but as a member of the West Side Oilfields Recreation District and as a writer for the *Taft Midway Driller*. "Tom was the sports editor for the local newspaper, wrote almost all the articles relating to sports in the community, helped develop many community sports activities and probably contributed more to sports in Taft than anyone," according to Lawrence "Larry" Peahl, who had been a high school teammate of Patterson, and years later was an administrator at Taft College where he also coached the track team. O'Brien was arguably an exceptional coach, with a list of other outstanding Taft throwers — Archie Schmitt, Mike Garrett, Richard Russell, and Patrick Young — to his credit. "It was all about speed, technique and attention to detail," explained Peahl. "Tom would be with them in every move they made in the rings."

Like Leon's biological father, O'Brien was a compact man. Unlike him, he was a devout Catholic and an equally devoted family man, who exemplified moderation and who inspired confidence. Leon's Taft contemporary, Dave Hollingsworth, who became the nation's leading prep hurdler in 1954 and later a USC Trojan, recalled, "I think the most influential coach at Taft was Tom O'Brien, who was the weight coach but helped us all with his strong support. He helped in my running when he suggested that I train with a baton, which he said 'gave me cadence.' One great guy."

Tom had originally met Leon when the husky boy was 14 and the only freshman playing varsity football. O'Brien kept his eye on the youngster, since Leon seemed to epitomize that magic word for high school coaches — "potential." He was, as well, not a kid who needed to brag, and O'Brien also appreciated that. As Leon sprinted and jumped in dual and triangular meets his sophomore year, Tom worked with him on weight techniques. At first Patterson — thrusting with his arm but not his legs — barely put the shot over 40 feet, then over 42, then over 44, all the while learning to use his legs and his body's momentum to propel the 12-pound metal ball.

Spinning the discus made his speed more obvious to observers, although in that event, too, he had to learn to control his velocity. One practice throw with the platter might flutter 90 feet, the next travel 120, then the next veer only 110 as he fought to develop consistency. His natural quickness was difficult to control on sandy shot and discus rings at Taft, and more experienced athletes with less talent were ahead of him early in the season but, encouraged by O'Brien and Voorhees, Leon didn't quit.

By midseason, Leon was improving his marks notably with each competition. He was also consistently scoring points in the 100-yard dash, the broad jump, and in the sprint relay. One of his rivals in the weights, Dewey Sceales of East Bakersfield High School, knew that Patterson was really just a beginner, if a well-coached one. Sceales was, as a result, amazed when Leon managed to "catch a throw just right" and fling the discus into the bleachers at EBHS. The toss couldn't be measured, so the rumor started that Leon had broken "the high school world record."

In fact, Patterson for a long while remained inconsistent with the discus because he had trouble controlling his speed. He was more steady in the shot put, where he also edged out not only Sceales but also Bakersfield High's Pat Foutch, who later said Patterson's improvement from one meet to the next was phenomenal. At O'Brien's urging, Leon studied the form of more experienced putters and throwers such as Sceales, Foutch, and Bakersfield's Hugh Hearndon, and near the end of his sophomore season he had improved to 51 feet 7 inches in the shot put to qualify for the California State High School Championships — then considered the nation's premier high school meet.

O'Brien and Patterson continued tweaking the Wildcat's technique, and Foutch much later told John Pryor that Patterson's putting stance became unorthodox, with the shot held a few inches away rather than tucked under his chin as was the common approach. It must have worked since at Sacramento's Hughes Stadium that year Leon continued to study his opponents during the competition, to learn from them, and to surprise them: On his final put; he sent the shot 53 feet 11 inches for third place, shattering Taft High School's quite respectable school record previously held by Dick Snyder. Tom O'Brien knew that bringing home that bronze medal was just the beginning for Leon.

His opponents had been studying the Taft thrower, too, since at 5 feet 11 inches and under 180 pounds, he seemed too small for his accomplishments, although he was by far the most explosive medalist. A few foes suggested that he must be "taking something" that aided his success. Told that, one ex-teammate laughed and said, "Yeah, he was taking Tom O'Brien's coaching." That was, in any case, the last time Leon Patterson ever lost a competition in the high school throws.

Since the National AAU Decathlon Championships were being contested at the end of June just 75 miles up the road in Tulare, hometown of Olympic champion Bob Mathias, Taft's coaches thought that entering the meet might be a chance to assess Leon's potential in that 10-event ordeal. Leon was more than a little awestruck as he found himself in the company of world class decathletes such as Bill Albans, Floyd Simmons, Otey Scruggs and the gracious Mathias, who seemed to be the hero of every Central Valley schoolboy, and who encouraged Leon after meeting him, treating him like an old pal.

Some of Leon's teammates in attendance remember that the more experienced, world-class decathletes were warming up for the high jump wearing sweat clothes, and easily sailing over heights well beyond Leon's best. Leon just grinned and shook his head. Taft boosters, of course, underestimated the quality of the competition Patterson would be facing, and overestimated what Leon's raw talent might accomplish, so were disappointed when he scored only 4,896 points and finished toward the rear of the pack, while the remarkable Mathias set a new world record with 8,042 points.

Leon had taken nearly a month off after the state high school championship meet, doing little or no training, especially on unfamiliar events like the hurdles or the javelin. He performed poorly in those competitions, but remained in the mix — if below par — in the 16-pound shot, where he put 44 feet 4 inches, and in the international discus (heavier than the scholastic discus), with a throw of 127 feet 2 inches. He was well off his best in the broad jump at 19 feet and the high jump at 5 feet 6 inches; he almost didn't finish when he started much too fast and tied up in the 400-meter dash, and the 1,500-meter run was for him torture. It was not only a lesson in humility for the high school star, but also confirmed what coach O'Brien had been telling him about the importance of technique, sharpness, and conditioning.

"At least," Leon said afterward, "I got to meet Bob Mathias." That initial decathlon was one more lesson for a young man who was learning a great deal about everything from table manners to social behavior to training diets. In those years, most prep weight men, especially shot putters, tended to be big lugs, ponderous but strong. Patterson was more like another of his heroes, world discus record holder Fortune Gordien, compact and swift. Like Gordien, his speed in the discus circle could be dazzling, and of course he was surprisingly strong, pumping out one-handed push-ups in practice until Dixie lost count.

Elvin Urquhart remained a pal, as well as a source of transportation. The two young men did extra training near Elvin's residence. Leon "would often stay at my house," Elvin recollected. "Coach unofficially 'loaned' us some hurdles, and Leon and I would have our own practice at my house, including shot put and discus followed by a BBQ. The only event I could beat him in was the hurdles," said Urquhart, who lived "in the middle of nowhere at Belridge in the oilfields. We had miles of open space to train on," added Urquhart. "Leon, he would often stay overnight. He was quiet, shy and polite around my parents," added Elvin. "My 10-year-old brother was in awe of his prowess."

In the football-crazy San Joaquin Valley, Leon's grid potential intrigued many fans awaiting the season of 1950 even more than did his throwing ability. He had run the 100-yard dash in 10.3 seconds with no special training, contributing to the success of Taft's sprint relay team. He was also the strongest player on the football team, and agile

— noted for hurdling would-be tacklers. Charlie Hanna remembers that Leon intimidated defensive backs; "By about the second quarter they'd be backing up, hoping he'd run the other way. He was the best high school running back I ever saw, and I saw both Gayle Sayers and Marcus Allen."

Elvin Urquhart added one more tidbit: "After home football games at Taft High, kids would occasionally meet at a shutdown WWII military airport, Gardner Field, and build bonfires, sip beer, and perhaps drag race. Leon and various buddies would then throw empty beer kegs, ostensibly as ad hoc practice for the shot put or discus." Elvin did not specify how the kegs were emptied or by whom, but Leon won that event too.

Eight

By the beginning of the school year 1950-51, Leon and his pals were young men. Many owned (or otherwise had access to) cars of their own and, like him, many had steady girlfriends. Drivers licenses were then available in California for 16-year-olds, so the use of cars changed the lives of youngsters in and around relatively remote towns like Taft and much enhanced the kids' senses of the possible. Also, like small-town boys all over the country, they took their adventures where they could find them. For instance, Elvin Urquhart remembered that he and Leon "would go rabbit hunting in my dad's 1939 grocery delivery van. The shooter would straddle the passenger side headlight and we would take off across the desert chasing rabbits," he reported. It was both illegal and dangerous, which made it just right for teenage adventurers.

They could also embark on drives to (or at least toward) urban Southern California, or through the beautiful and largely unsettled Cuyama Valley just southwest of Taft, where range cattle roamed just as they had in the days of Spanish settlement, or to the even more remote Carriso Plain where sand-hill cranes gathered seasonally at Soda Lake, or perhaps to the out-of-the-way Carneros Rocks on Twisselman Ranch in the hills west of town.

Some Taft kids ventured completely over the western hills to California's central coast, to settings like Pismo, Avila, Oceano, Arroyo Grande, Morro Bay, etc. — a tourist's dream and one of the state's more beautiful regions. The coast was a long, long way from the Westside desert, conceptually if not physically. Closer to home, of course, young lovers explored other mysteries on Hill 25, the local teenagers' favorite make-out locale. (Some local wags referred to it as "makers' acres.") Only the Sunset Drive-In Theater in Ford City just east of Taft rivaled Hill 25 as a youthful romantic rendezvous. Taft Beach, a sandy stretch near where the Kern River crossed the road to Wasco, was another nearby favorite locale.

Unfortunately, that new decade, the 1950s, brought with it at least one unanticipated challenge: the Korean War. It may have been passed off by some politicians as a "police action," but for the young men who would be conscripted to fight, and to their families, it was a war. A few kids who had played high school football with or against Leon would soon find themselves in mortal combat. Taft was locally famous (or infamous) for its nearly all-white population, so notice was also taken there when a one-time UCLA athlete and a United Nations' peacekeeper, Dr. Ralph Bunche, became the first African American to win a Nobel Peace Prize, symbolizing the ongoing, gradual change in racial relationships that was underway in America...even in Kern County.

Leon was known as a straight arrow — a good guy — by his classmates. He was also remembered as an athlete whose sportsmanship included "the same handshake for the colored boy as his white opponent." George Patterson, with some pride, described his youngest sibling as "unlike anyone else in the family in that he was very outgoing, made friends easier than us. Very determined and self-confident, and of course, he was extremely strong physically. I remember in his circle of friends, he was always the strongest and fastest."

He was not in the least a bully or a troublemaker, according to his peers. Cork Donnell, who stood only 5 feet 5 inches and weighed little more than 100 pounds, recalled that his girlfriend had a class with Leon, who would walk with her from building to building. "It started aggravating me, and people were talking," Cork recalled. "I had a talk with Leon and told him he would have to stop walking her to class. He understood and quit." Cork later told Leon Patterson, Jr., that "he had been scared to death, thought my dad was going to beat him up. I think my dad thought Cork was a stand-up man."

That fall a new head football coach, Bob Hoffman, took the reins at Taft Union High School. It was Leon's junior year, and hopes were high indeed for a stellar gridiron season. Many players were returning including potential all-leaguers like Ray Herman, Gary Green, Elvie Dalton, and Patterson — each of whom loomed large in the coaches' plans. The team's four-win, five-loss season that included a 0-44 thumping at the hands of Merced disappointed everyone. One bright spot, Dixie later recollected, was the "chaperoned dances in the gym" after games. "As we would dance around the floor, people would congratulate Leon."

He was no longer merely that fast kid from Derby Acres, but was one of the veterans, buddies with Dalton and Hanna, Green and Herman, and all the rest. He was also voted the team's Most Valuable Player and, despite the Wildcats' unimpressive record, he became the subject of interest from college coaches.

Dixie didn't at all mind being the girlfriend of a gridiron star. "After football games he would shower and I cleaned up in the food booth where I usually worked. Then we would meet and go out to the drive-in for a coke. While the games were on and we weren't busy. I could watch Leon hurdle the pack and run for touchdowns. I was really proud of him."

All the while, young Mr. Patterson was also becoming an ever more permanent fixture in the Kenney family, just as he and Dixie were more and more thought of at school as a couple. He had by then obtained use of a 1941 "torpedo back" Pontiac belonging to his brother Calvin. It ran well but could only be started by pushing, so Leon became an expert at parking on slopes. Dixie also recalled that "it wasn't unusual to be in a formal dress pushing the car, with Leon in a suit, to go to a prom." Then she added, "We kind of got used to it."

One weekend he and Dixie ventured in the Pontiac out Route 166 to the thinly settled Cuyama Valley for a picnic. They found a "nice grassy field with big shade trees," so they parked, then Leon crawled over and Dixie crawled through a fence, found a comfortable location, and spread out an old blanket. "I got out the fried chicken, potato salad, and Kool-Aid," Dixie remembered. "We were enjoying our meal when we heard a sound...like a snort." They glanced around and saw "looking mighty unpleasant, tossing dirt here and there...a big black bull." Leon grabbed the blanket by all four corners and scooped up the food, and the couple sprinted back to the fence, which both hurdled. "Luckily, the bull stopped at the fence. Leon looked at me and I at him and we both laughed so hard we almost cried." As Leon Patterson, Jr., much later heard the story, his father had not only hurdled the fence grasping the blanket but with a half-eaten chicken leg clasped in his teeth.

The course of young love didn't necessarily always run smoothly for Dixie and Leon. For instance, that summer Leon joined the Kenney family at their campsite on Bass Lake. Dixie and Leon were at the local store and boat dock, and "Leon was showing off on the diving board and the girls as usual were flocked around him," reported Dixie, "So I grabbed a boy I knew, and we rowed way out in the lake.

The next thing I knew, Leon had caught up with us swimming and pulled himself into the boat. He took the oars away from the boy and rowed us back to the dock. I didn't speak to him the rest of the day."

They also broke up more than once, she later reported, but she only dated one other boy at Taft High after meeting Leon, Riley Jones, who "came from a military academy and didn't know much about the kids at school," she explained. Leon had let word out that no one had better date "his" Dixie even when they weren't steadies, but Riley didn't get the message. Little matter, since as Dixie explained, "We always went back together mostly because we seemed to be made for each other, and we were both miserable apart."

In the off-season Leon continued working on his techniques in the throwing events with Tom O'Brien. The latter was jocularly described as Leon's "unfair advantage" by retired attorney Charles Werdel, who in the 1950s put the shot for one of Taft's rivals, Garces Memorial High School. Says Werdel, "Personally, I know that he [O'Brien] would help any young man up and down the San Joaquin Valley who would drive to Taft. Tom O'Brien spent many late afternoons and weekends working with me and never asked for any form of compensation whatsoever." In particular, Werdel remembers coach O'Brien suggesting to him that he "keep his left shoulder straight to generate more power. I went from being a 55-foot thrower to 58-plus feet. He seemed to understand the physics of throwing, and he was a generous man." Mike Butcher, a shot putter at Bakersfield High School, who eventually became track coach at West Bakersfield High School, described O'Brien as "a truly gifted weight coach."

Little wonder Leon not only developed confidence in himself, but also confidence in his coach. Their close relationship was obvious to all. Werdel observed simply, "They were buddies." O'Brien's daughter, Lynne, later explained that "Tom and Leon could communicate without talking," not that they didn't talk. As they worked together more and more, Tom slowly became Patterson's primary male role model and his confidante. Leon was a lucky young man indeed to have such a mentor. As for O'Brien, he recognized that Patterson was a smart kid, so he explained what was necessary and the two of them continued working on harnessing the athlete's speed. They also experimented with adjustments to conventional techniques: raising or lowering the shoulders, holding the shot a bit away from his neck, limiting or increasing the knee bend when throwing the discus. "It was all about speed, technique, attention to detail," recalls Larry Peahl. "Tom would be with them in every move they made in the ring."

Patterson began the season of 1951 by winning six events in Taft High School's Interclass Meet: 100-yard dash, high jump, pole vault, broad jump, shot put, and discus. His 21-foot broad jump especially surprised coaches since he had done no training for that event. Talk of him as a natural decathlete once again heated up. Moreover, his marks for the weight events immediately showed what he'd accomplished thanks to O'Brien's coaching and his own dedication: He opened the season with 55 feet 1 inch in the shot, 157 feet in the discus. By the time he met serious competition at Santa Barbara's Easter Relays, he put the 12-pound high school shot 56 feet 6½ inches; with the 16-pound collegiate shot, he managed a startling 49 feet 10¾ inches, and he also threw the high school discus 150 feet 10 inches.

One highlight of the track season occurred at the Kern County Track Meet held in Taft's Martin Memorial Stadium. Not only was Leon the favorite in both weight events, which he won handily, he was also an important runner on Taft's sprint relay team. Dixie was also a Meet Princess, and she was scheduled to award medals to second, third, fourth, and fifth placers in various events. Shirley Cummins, the queen, would award all gold medals. Dixie remembered:

When it came time to award first place to Leon, the queen handed me his trophy and told me to give it to him. He was on the highest riser. I reached up to hand him the trophy, which he took in one hand, and with his other arm he grabbed me around my waist and lifted me up on the riser and kissed me. I turned 10 shades of red, and the crowd cheered and clapped.

In May, Leon easily won his events at the prestigious West Coast Relays in Fresno, then did the same at the Yosemite League Championships, and at the Central CIF "Masters' Meet" — as the regional semi-final for the state championships was called. He was still improving steadily, and his marks in that competition established two new records: 58 feet 2¾ inches in the shot put, 166 feet 6 inches in the discus. At the state championship in Berkeley the following week, he set a state 12-pound shot put record of 59 feet 2½ inches, becoming only the third Californian to exceed 59 feet. He also won the discus with 165 feet 5 inches, well under his seasonal best of 173 feet 9 inches, and won the nonscoring 16-pound shot at 48 feet. (There was a small irony at those meets since many spectators saw the new sensation for the first time, and some later admitted they had expected him to be African American. Taft, of course, was locally reputed to be all-white.)

Standing atop the victory stand in Edwards Stadium on the University of California's campus to receive the award for his shot put victory, he was again the smallest medalist. Dixie recalled that Leon grinned modestly and waved to the crowd, then he saw her and winked. It was one of those special moments between them that she never forgot. He had every reason to be proud for he had not only just vanquished previously unbeaten Clyde Wetter of Grossmont High School, but had also just become the number one rated prep weight man in the nation. Buoyed by his improvement that season, Leon confided in Tom O'Brien that his goals were to put the high school shot over 60 feet and then to throw the college discus over 200 feet. Coach O'Brien agreed that both those objectives were attainable for him.

Leon Patterson was not only a rare triple champion at the 1951 California State High School Track and Field Championships, but was also named the national Prep Athlete of the Year by *Track & Field News*, the sport's defining publication. This was considered the highest honor a high-school "thin clad" could earn. Leon, of course, remained a prime college recruit for football as well as track. Moreover, Leon had by then managed to climb into the upper half of his class academically, so coaches from all over the country were contacting him. He was flattered and a little dazzled, too, with the likes of Notre Dame, USC, and UCLA urging him to consider their football programs.

NINE

Taft had always been a working-class community, full of families that supported education and sought upward mobility for their kids. As a result, it offered wholesome outlets beyond interscholastic sports — such as that busy recreation center, a well-stocked library, and a large indoor swimming center. Historically, though, Taft and the small, oilfield communities surrounding it, had also been known as a hard place where men young and old tested their masculinity in direct physical confrontations. The town's police chief in 1976, Walter McKee, observed, "Taft is notorious rough country. This is an oil town. Heck, we have a dozen fights some nights."

A clash of cultures triggered by the Southwestern migration led to more than a few street fights in the period from the 1930s through the 1950s: new arrivals would not allow themselves to be denigrated by longer-term Californians. James Gregory in *American Exodus: The Dust*

Bowl Migration and Okie Culture in California, entitles a section of his book "Cult of Toughness," noting that "persistence was more than the key to success — there could be no dignity, manhood or self-respect without it." As a result, "a preoccupation with toughness became one of the cornerstones of the Okie subculture." He might well have added "Arkie" and "Texie," or perhaps employed the more general word "migrant," when he concluded, "Toughness also meant a willingness to fight."

Leon Patterson and his buddies were typical Taft teens by 1951, not always employing sound judgment, looking for adventures wherever they might find them, so they had a few scraps, both locally and in nearby Bakersfield. That city, the county seat, housed three rival high schools — Bakersfield, East Bakersfield, and Garces — as well as several teen hangouts like drive-in restaurants and both indoor and outdoor movie theaters, as well as various other venues for dining or entertainment, so it was often a first choice for out-of-town adventures.

Dick Henning recalls more than once joining Leon and other TUHS jocks at Bakersfield's Rainbow Gardens dance hall, where they might hear the music of everyone from Bill Woods to Fats Domino. "Going there to dance on Saturday nights was always a little risky because we were athletic rivals with Bakersfield," recalls Henning. Local rumors had it that Rainbow Gardens had hosted more bouts than Madison Square Garden. "More often than not, we would end up in the parking lot in fist fights," recalls Henning, "which we loved because we could brag about them on Mondays at school."

The Taft crew had other tricks up their sleeves — or in their pants — as it turned out. Explains Henning:

> *The young men of Bakersfield were mostly farmers, ranchers or cowboys; so in order to compete for the girls, we would stop at a vegetable stand on the highway a couple of miles from Rainbow Gardens and*

each of us would buy a potato, which we stuck into our jockey shorts. We asked girls to dance, never paying attention whether they were with big husky boyfriends or not, and this often ended in disaster, but we did impress a lot of young women with our potatoes.

One experiment employing a large zucchini went awry, however, and led to a car chase from Rainbow Gardens on the outskirts of Bakersfield toward Taft. When only one car with three guys in it remained in pursuit, the four Taft worthies being chased pulled over and fisticuffs ensued. While six boys were engaged in a three-on-three brawl, Henning "sneaked around to their car, and let the air out of all four tires." The Taft crew soon departed leaving their erstwhile opponents stranded some 15 miles from home. It made for a grand story at school on Monday.

Another battle had less humorous consequences. After Leon had become known as a special athlete, some oil workers decided to put the kid in his place. A group of them, four or five, according to Leon's brother Calvin — and "probably beered up" — jumped Leon and gave him a thumping. The young jock returned home and told Calvin what had happened, then the two Patterson brothers sought out the aggressors one at a time over a period of days, forcing each to fight Leon one-on-one. All were badly beaten and none requested a rematch. The Pattersons' minor crusade became well known locally, but no one interceded on behalf of the miscreants. The local code called for one-on-one fights, and they had broken it, so few if any offered them sympathy.

On the classier end of out-of-town social events, "We did go to Maison Jaussaud's French restaurant in Bakersfield after the prom," recalls Elvin Urquhart. "That was the ultimate." Less swishy, perhaps, but also possibly more fun, were trips to Strelich's Stadium in Bakersfield, a boxing and wrestling arena that drew large crowds each week when professional wrestlers drove up from Southern California to put on a show. Urquhart transported a gang there from Taft, only to learn that adult chaperones were required if teenagers were to attend. No problem, since all the guys gave their money to Leon — who was their age but looked older — and he was able to buy tickets for everyone. He could also usually buy beer when that was the order of the day.

Ninth-grader David Hollingsworth was a new teammate of Patterson's at TUHS that year; he would eventually become a standout prep high hurdler. Academic standards at Taft High were rigorously enforced, so rather than simply pass star athletes, faculty members made certain that they achieved genuine acceptable standards. In order to qualify for college, and to be eligible for athletic competition, Dave took an algebra class with upper-classman Leon, who was still compensating for earlier academic deficiencies. Ed Sewell, a former football coach, was their instructor and, recalled Hollingsworth, "Ed wanted to make sure Leon survived algebra and would keep him after class to tutor him. I would just join in. Leon was a hard-working student who would continually tell Ed how much he appreciated the extra help. We both passed."

Hollingsworth had another memorable experience with Patterson that year. "As a freshman," he explains:

I went out for track and specifically the sprints. Les Voorhees was our coach. At our first time trials, I was lined up next to Leon. I thought it was strange knowing he was a shot putter and discus thrower. Leon ran 10.4 seconds, and I ran 10.5 at 100 yards. After that I figured I better find another event if I couldn't beat the weight team. To make a long story short, I switched to the hurdles and as a senior ran 14.3, which is still the Taft HS record and was the top time in the country in 1954.

Another of Leon's track teammates was old buddy Elvin Urquhart, who had by then acquired a 6-cylinder 1939 Plymouth he believed could beat any V8 at school at the various informal drag races that might erupt at places like Gardner Field. Fortunately, Elvin and Leon remained close:

> One day at high school I noticed that my '39 Plymouth coupe was missing my prize full-moon hub caps. When I spotted them on the car of a tough scrapper, I enlisted Leon to help me retrieve the hub caps. As Leon took a large screwdriver to the stolen hub caps, the thieves just watched from some distance. My hub caps were safe after that.

Shortly thereafter, though, Leon nearly got Dixie in a bit of trouble in high school. She was a "goody-goody" who had never ditched class, but one day he managed to talk her into trying it. She pretended to be ill, then met Leon and they drove to the coast (to Morro Bay or Pismo, she couldn't remember which) where they "had a lovely walk on the beach and fish lunch and started back." On the trip to Taft, however, a rainstorm struck and the windshield wipers on Leon's brother's clunker of a car didn't work, "so we took turns running outside to use my P.E. towel to wipe off the windows. It was horrible," she later wrote. "We did make it back and I vowed I'd never do that again. I always felt guilty about it." Leon thought it was funny.

Like his chums, he also got a kick out of defrauding the Sunset Drive-In Theater, where Elvin and another pal, Bud Nestell, worked. Recalls Urquhart, "All the kids came. Leon and Dixie sometimes, and Leon with the boys sometimes. Bud would ask 'How many?' seeing at least ten and the driver would say 'Six.'" Dixie also remembered that when she and Leon went to the drive-in alone, and neither Bud nor Elvin were on duty, just for the fun of it Leon often insisted on climbing into the car's trunk in order to sneak in even if they had plenty of money for the fare.

By then the young couple had grown close indeed, but still hadn't "gone all the way" due to Dixie's insistence that they save sexual intercourse for marriage. Petting and necking, however, were frequent and intense indulgences.

Secret kisses or intimate squeezes even in the hallway of the school were private delights, as were parking sessions on Hill 25 or other oilfield locales, or at the drive-in movie.

Leon also seemed to much enjoy being treated as a family member by the Kenneys. As Dixie told it, "Once he showed up while I was white-washing the house." Always eager to help, but also practical, "Leon was soon climbing up the ladder with a pail and brush. He knew the sooner we got the stucco house painted white, the sooner we'd be able to go out, so he helped." Dixie's parents wisely invited Leon to join Dixie on many family outings, something that not only kept the kids out of trouble and that Leon much appreciated, since his own family offered little or nothing in the way of social gatherings. Everything from picnics to camping trips were shared by the Kenneys with him, and he had by 1951 begun to feel he was part of their family. Dixie's mother would gently boss him around as though he were her third child, and Leon seems always to have obeyed with good humor.

One outing in particular seemed to Dixie to summarize the family's excursions. She didn't remember the exact date, but they were staying at Pismo State Beach when she taught Leon how to clam. "He loved it and wanted to continue long after we all got our limits." However, "Leon didn't think cleaning the clams was nearly as much fun as getting them, but he liked eating fried clams." Her mother, who ruled the kitchen, "would have Leon and I grind the tougher clams with an old hand grinder and then she would make clam chowder out of them."

Another grinder — thoroughly washed — was used for an additional family tradition: making cranberry relish for Thanksgiving and Christmas dinners. "Leon would turn the handle for me, and we would grind the cranberries, apples, and oranges together." That task was a tradition of long standing in the Kenney family. "He thought it was pretty nice. We all sang around the piano which I played and Dad played his violin. We sang Christmas carols, drank egg nog, cracked nuts, and I guess in general were like most families," or like most families she'd previously known, anyway. Dixie had always taken the closeness of her own household for granted...until she met Leon. His response led her to observe, "I don't think he ever experienced the closeness of family before ours. He practically lived with us while we were going together."

Leon had good reason to avoid home, one that he kept secret, as she would later learn: his father's drinking and uncontrolled outbursts of rage. Dolores O'Brien told Earl Gustkey in 1991 that Leon came by the O'Brien house early one morning, when he was in his junior year at the high school and asked to talk to Tom outside:

> He told Tom that his father had been drunk all night and had beaten him up. Well, I think Tom just laughed at first. Then he saw that Leon was serious. Leon's father was half his size. Leon could have squashed him like an ant.
>
> But, apparently, he'd never touched his father during this long altercation. Then Leon asked Tom if it would be okay if he moved in with us. Tom and I talked about it but decided against it. We later told him he should stay at home and try to work out problems, not run away from them.
>
> Well, we've thought about that many times over the years and sometimes we would second-guess ourselves. After all these years, I still wonder if in the hour of his greatest need, we'd failed him.

The sad truth is that they might have.

Much later, Dixie wrote in her unpublished memoir, "Leon never told me about his dad beating him up. I did notice how subdued his mother was around his father, trying hard to please him. At the time I wondered if he abused her."

Leon, Taft Union High School Graduation – 1952.

Leon pole vaulting at the National AAU decathlon championship in 1951. Tom O'Brien at right prepares to catch the pole.

*Taft High sprint relay team 1952.
Leon second from left.*

Taft High yearbook photo of Leon throwing the discus.

In his senior year at Taft High, 1952, Leon (far right), along with a cadre of classmates, drove south to Long Beach one weekend, visited the boardwalk, and all got the same tattoos on their right biceps, a rebellious act indeed in those distant days. Others are (left to right), Gary Green, Elvin Urquhart, and Elvie Dalton.

The Wedding Party, June 20, 1953

Left to right: Gail McCabe, Jeanine Garrison, Patricia Dykes, Dixie Leon, Tom O'Brien, Maurice Kenney.
Flower girls: Suzanne and Richelle Dykes.

Taft's social event of the summer of 1953 was the wedding of Dixie Kenney to Leon Patterson.

Dixie used her savings to put a down payment on a 1953 black Pontiac Catalina hardtop as a wedding gift to Leon.

Leon was the nation's leading freshman discus thrower for USC in 1953.

Orel Leon "Lee" Patterson, Jr., with son Orel Leon Patterson III. According to family sources, "Leon O. Patterson" was used on the tombstone because it was the late athlete's chosen name.

TEN

Leon was delighted to have been offered a summer job in the oilfields, where work would be steady and the pay was good. He would begin as a roustabout — a general helper — and had only to go through the formalities, which included a physical exam, before being issued a hardhat and a locker. To the astonishment of nearly everyone, Dolores O'Brien later explained, after the physical examination, "We learned that albumen had shown up in his urine, and the doctor told him that he had Bright's disease [Glomerulonephritis], and that he was fatally ill." Dolores continued:

> He came to our house that night, just burst through the door. He told us a doctor had told him he was going to die. He was in tears, and we just couldn't believe it. I mean he was a big, strong, healthy looking kid. Tom was furious with the doctor, and he took Leon and went out to see him first thing the next morning.

> *Tom started to chew out this doctor, and the doctor quickly took Tom in another room, away from Leon. He told him firmly that he felt Leon had about two years to live.*

Dixie's memory of hearing the news from Leon was stark: "He came to me that night. We went out on a date, but we just parked and talked for hours. He started to cry...told me he would die in 10 years," and she was ready to marry him immediately, for at that instant marriage seemed to be the only way to help the boy she loved. Although there would certainly be some light moments ahead for them, some future adventures, and some flashes of joy, their lives would never again be the same, and both Dixie and Leon sensed that. Whether he lived 10 years or 2, they would survive together. The affirmation that followed would be both their strength and their burden; break-ups over small disagreements were over. Long before taking their formal wedding vows, until death do us part became their commitment.

Tom O'Brien and Monty Reedy called Dr. Leon Goldman in San Francisco, and the noted physician made room in his busy schedule to examine Leon. A Taft native, Dr. Goldman (whose daughter, Dianne Feinstein, later became a U.S. Senator from California), practiced urology at the University of California, San Francisco. Coach Reedy drove Leon north and tried to remain upbeat about the enhanced treatments that might be possible at a major medical center like UCSF. Unfortunately, tests there confirmed the diagnosis of Bright's disease, and X-rays also revealed that Patterson had only one large, horseshoe-shaped kidney that was "in a rapid state of disintegration." Goldman warned Leon that continuing to play football, in particular, would hasten the disease's progress.

George Patterson spoke for many when he said, "I don't think any of us, including Leon, ever fully accepted that he was dying. My God, if you'd just seen him — he looked like he could bend a crowbar. We just believed that somehow he would beat this thing. I know I just put it out of my mind." On a rational level, though, the people with whom the information was shared had at some point to acknowledge its reality, as much as they hated doing that, but only a small group initially knew the truth. When Leon informed his coach and teammates that he could not play football the next season they were stunned; he looked well and more than well. He said he didn't have time for the gridiron because he had to raise his grades in order to go to college; then he told others he was ill, but did not tell them how ill or about his prognosis. What had been projected as a championship team at Taft lost at least three starters that year, including Dale Stineberg, killed in a hunting accident; Fred Snyder relocated to Fresno with his family and, of course, Leon left due to illness. The school's yearbook would say, "The Taft Wildcats were mishandled by Lady Luck."

Dixie informed her parents of Leon's condition, and they took it hard; he had become their boy, too. The young man's prognosis wasn't easy for any of the Kenneys to accept and deal with. What would Dixie do? It had been assumed that she and Leon would marry after high school, but now even that was up in the air. She was willing to quit school and marry him immediately, but her teachers and family alike urged her to graduate, and Leon agreed.

Everyone who knew Leon's prognosis hoped that he'd be granted at least the 10 years one doctor had supposedly said was possible. In 10 years, a cure might be found, or at least a treatment. In 10 years anything might be possible. George Patterson described his younger brother's attitude as "very determined and self-confident."

When coaches asked him if he wanted to try another decathlon, Leon said yes. He was more than a little distracted trying to come to grips with what he had learned about his health, but he and Tom O'Brien drove to Santa Barbara so he could compete in the National AAU Decathlon Championships there. Ever since Central Valley neighbor

Bob Mathias had won the 1948 Olympic gold medal in the event, decathlon had been a high profile competition in California. Bob's younger brother Jim, who competed for Tulare High School and who was a friendly rival of Leon's, was another entry, but Patterson seemed, on paper at least, to be the most formidable high school competitor.

In fact, although his coaches wanted to keep him busy so he wouldn't dwell on what he'd heard from doctors, he did only light training for events that were relatively new to him, such as the high hurdles, the 400 meters, and the 1,500 meters. As a result, the hurdles were again disaster for his chances, and he once more started much too fast in the 400-meter dash and slowed considerably in the homestretch, yet his competitive marks in the 100 meters, the broad jump, and the javelin indicated his considerable potential. And he posted the best marks of any entrant in the 16-pound shot put of 47 feet 9⅝ inches and the international discus of 149 feet 4 inches against several of the world's best decathletes, including Floyd Simmons, Otey Scruggs, and the Rev. Bob Richards; the latter won the competition. Leon finished ninth overall with 6,395 points. If he had time, it was clear that he could become a world-class decathlete — his score indicated that he was already close to that level — but no one could be certain if he had time.

When the next school year began, Dixie said, she "stopped my academic course, kept my business course and took home economics. I knew I was going to marry Leon and thought I should learn how to cook and sew." As seemed consistently true of her, Dixie excelled at her new curriculum, and would eventually be presented the Bank of America Award for outstanding home economics graduate when she received her diploma in 1953. By then her plans to marry Leon and to work to put him through school were well established. According to Elvin Urquhart, Leon had by then also begun sleeping most nights at the O'Brien house.

For the two young people, though, the terrible threat posed by Bright's disease almost immediately moved their relationship into full sexual intimacy. "I guess I thought it would help us some way," Dixie recalled. "We were both virgins. He was nervous, I was calm. After that, whenever our two busy schedules permitted, we would park and be together."

She also recalled that one day when they had driven to the mostly deserted oil fields —where dirt roads criss-crossed other dirt roads, and where privacy could usually be enjoyed even in midday. An oil worker who was checking pumps happened upon them when they were mostly unclothed, *en flagrante delicto*, and "Leon was furious and wanted to beat him up," recalled Dixie, "but I talked him into jumping into the front seat and getting us out of there while I dressed in the back seat." As they sped away, a fully clothed Dixie crawled from the rear seat to the front, and Leon laughed, saying, "I bet the old guy was jealous. So I laughed, too."

Some of Leon's pals, who'd heard he was ill, but didn't know how ill or with what, noticed that he wasn't as often available for adventures, and tended to blame Dixie, whom they assumed was "controlling." The high school term "pussy whipped" was mumbled, but not in Leon's presence.

When Patterson did sneak out with the guys, though, he was as rambunctious as ever. The shock of diagnosis and prognosis remained on some level unbelievable, so Leon could still be something of a rascal. During fall of 1951, for instance, Dick Henning and Leon ventured to the Rainbow Gardens to dance with Bakersfield girls and drink some beer. When the hall closed, they drove back toward Taft, but decided it would be better to sleep first, so they pulled off on a dirt track amidst cotton fields. "We woke up about 5 a.m. and spotted one of the huge, meshed-wire cotton trailers sitting in the field full of picked cotton. We drove over to the truck, and each of us grabbed a long cotton sack and filled it about three-quarters full. We hid the sacks in a dry riverbed a few hundred yards down the field of unpicked cotton."

When the workers arrived at about 7 a.m., the two athletes stood in line and received empty sacks, then began walking up and down rows pulling bolls of cotton and dropping them in the sacks. "Within an hour of picking," Henning continued, "I had scratches on the lower part of my arms from the dried leaves, and I was convinced my bag had a hole in it. My shoulders ached. My legs ached. My arms ached. My fingers ached." Meanwhile experienced pickers, including Leon, kept working without letup.

"We finally got to our hidden sacks, and we consolidated the bags with the cotton we had just picked and took the two full bags to the scales." The weighmaster paid Leon and Dick $12 total and complimented them on being fast workers. "He said, 'You guys are pretty good for white boys.'"

Another adventure that might have ended Leon's athletic career began innocently enough on a December night in 1951 when Leon, Henning, and Ron Amick were celebrating the beginning of Christmas vacation by "dragging Center Street" in Calvin Patterson's car. They drove to a favorite hangout, Abram's Drive-In at Ford City, but found it closed; they also found that the rear door had been left open. Henning later remembered that they "made sure we parked Leon's auto on the hill because we always had to push his car to get it started." Then Henning suggested, "Let's go in. I'll make us milkshakes," so they entered just as "a police spotlight shined through the windows. Leon ran for his car, and Ron and I ran across the street to hide in the bushes in front of the firehouse. The cop took off after Leon," so Ron and Dick went to Amick's house to sleep.

At about 2 a.m. a policeman arrived at the house and said, "We want to talk to these two boys. They were involved in a burglary tonight at Abram's Drive-In." Dick pleaded with the officer, saying, "The door was left open, and we didn't take anything."

"Please empty your pockets," ordered the policeman, and Amick handed him two rolls of pennies he had taken from the open cash register drawer. "We were going to jail for a $1 burglary," remembers Henning. Leon, who had just turned 18, was taken to the Kern County lockup in Bakersfield, while Amick and Henning were deposited at Kern County juvenile hall there. Eventually, Leon was moved to juvenile hall and all three spent Christmas behind bars.

Dixie recollected that "I was so afraid my parents would find out and never let me see Leon again." She added, "The Abrams were good people and dropped the charges and even took Leon into their home. Their daughter may have been behind it because she had a big crush on Leon." Later, Dixie's English teacher, Bailey Newly, called her to his office and she thought she "was really going to get it" for slacking off on her studies while Leon and his two cronies were in "juvie," but instead "he complimented me for sticking by Leon and said he realized it was a very hard thing for me to do."

If Dixie's parents didn't know about the arrest, they were likely the only folks in town who didn't. "Everyone at school had learned about our 'vacation,'" acknowledges Henning, because "we regaled them with stories, which included the fact that one of our jailmates was charged with murder." To the boys, it ended up just being another adventure.

Eleven

The ongoing war in Korea loomed as big news for most Americans in 1951, since the intervention of Chinese troops on the side of North Korea seemed to move all combatants closer to World War III. By midyear, fortunately, truce talks between North Korean and United Nations' representatives had begun and tensions had somewhat eased. In Philadelphia that June, the first computer built for commercial use, UNIVAC, was introduced, as was the first commercial color television and in November the first transcontinental direct-dial telephone service.

Still, in Taft, no news trumped or even mitigated what Leon had heard from doctors early the previous summer, but he continued to do his best not to dwell on it. Maybe, just maybe, the doctors were wrong. Or maybe a cure would be found before his condition grew worse. As stressful as that was, he at least had a girl who loved him, a mother who did all she could for him, and the beginnings of a support group with the Kenneys and the O'Briens, as well as his gang of pals from school, at its core.

During that summer, Leon and Dixie still escaped when they could to Taft Beach on the Kern River. "Leon was a good swimmer," his widow explained, "but he had no body fat and couldn't float. He had to power swim to keep up with me. I used to tease him because I floated like a cork." In those years before an upstream dam severely limited the river's flow, adventurers like Leon might also take advantage of a rope strung from a high tree, and sail out over relatively deep water, then bellow a Tarzan yell as the rope was released. "I'd tell him he was a Leo," Dixie said, so "he should roar like a lion, and so he did." Sometimes they'd meet pals there, barbecue hot dogs or marshmallows and drink soda or beer.

Dixie was by then involved in her home economics classes and remained highly competitive in girls' athletics. Her family continued its vacation travels to nearby camping areas principally on the central coast; if Leon wasn't working, he was always welcome to accompany them. He "loved kids," noted Dixie, "and they loved him. At the Pismo campground if I couldn't find Leon, he was usually off with a bunch of kids playing games."

He was still a kid himself in many ways, and that fall Leon was part of a group of Taft High rowdies who ventured to Bakersfield High School and burned a "T" on that archrival's lawn. During the football season of 1951, Patterson was working on his throwing techniques with the shot and discus with Tom O'Brien, but occasionally attended grid practice in his track clothes and acted as an unofficial assistant coach for younger players. He also occasionally disobeyed doctor's orders; recalls Neal McCabe, "by practicing with the varsity, carrying the ball, crashing powerfully through the line, without any pads, just wearing shorts and a T-shirt."

More than once, the coaching staff gasped at what they had lost when Leon had fallen ill. To them he looked vigorous, and he could outrun anyone on the team. He was still receiving calls from college football recruiters who hadn't heard that he wasn't playing, or who had heard and wondered why, and who found it difficult to accept what they heard when he or his coaches told them he was ill.

Basketball season saw Dixie and Leon among the sellout crowd that watched the Taft Wildcats win the school's first ever California Interscholastic Federation Central Section Basketball Championship. The underdog Wildcats, led by Leon's classmates Don Zumbro, Ray Herman and Charlie Hanna, as well as junior Ted Switzler, upset favored Edison Tech from Fresno 35-28. That victory initiated a rivalry that would be played out in two more Valley Championship games, won by Edison in 1955 (55-44) and Taft in 1956 (56-55). It was rendered more dramatic in that decade of increasing racial sensitivity by the fact that Taft's team was composed entirely of white players while Edison's was all black.

Throughout that season one college coach remained in nearly constant touch with Leon, and he was an unusual man. Jess Mortensen, of the University of Southern California, was an ex-All-American basketball player, who acted as both an assistant football coach and head track coach. The Trojans boasted the nation's strongest intercollegiate track and field program during his tenure — 1951 to 1961 — winning seven National Intercollegiate Athletic Association team championships in those eleven years. During that stretch, USC never lost a dual meet, going 64-0.

Mortensen had been told by Leon's coaches that the athlete had a kidney problem, but not its gravity or what they knew of his prognosis, not at first anyway. There was still a good deal of denial among Leon's family and friends, but he reportedly told coach Mortensen, "If there is something seriously wrong with me, I hope God will at least spare me until after the next Olympics."

The USC coach liked athletes such as Jon Arnett, Darryl Ellingson, Des Koch, and Jim Decker who could participate in more than one varsity sport. He also liked athletes who weren't full of themselves. Leon qualified on both counts. At first, too, Mortensen thought surely there was at least an outside chance that Patterson would recover his health and return to football, where his potential seemed unlimited. Throughout the 1951-52 school year, the Trojan coach stayed in touch with Leon, urging him to get his grades up and to keep them there so that he'd be eligible for an athletic scholarship.

Throughout that year, Leon practiced his different throwing techniques for the shot put and discus with determination. He was a naturally competitive person and was unwilling to ease up and perhaps give his competitors an edge. Dixie worked out with him during the off-season, helping however she could, while Tom O'Brien also showed up frequently to help Leon with his form. The discus can be an inconsistent event, since the platter is much affected by wind velocity and direction, as well as by the quality of the throwing ring. Dixie, many years later, claimed to have seen Leon break the interscholastic discus record twice. Once, she said, in a high school meet, the platter "landed in the stands and the judge said it couldn't count...they didn't have a long enough discus area. The other time was out by his house in the field where he practiced. Everything went just right and we measured over 203 feet."

With a death sentence hovering over him, Leon Patterson engaged that spring of 1952 in his epic shot put contest with Bill Nieder. That competition did a lot to keep his health out of his mind, as did the assurance from coach Mortensen that USC had a scholarship for him, football or no football. At the Easter Relays in Santa Barbara on April 12th, Leon pushed the high school shot a meet record 58 feet 1½ inches; then he came back to nearly upset national discus champion Fortune Gordien in the men's open 16-pound shot, 49 feet 10¾ inches to 49 feet 10¼ inches."

As they prepared for the Kern Relays that followed, Tom O'Brien told Leon that he'd buy him a steak dinner if he broke the 60-foot barrier with the 12-pound shot, only to be told by Leon that he'd never in his life eaten steak. He was about to enjoy one. Officials at the Kern Relays understood that Patterson was closing in on the national record, so special efforts were made to be certain all conditions were up to standards for the April 20th meet. Officials included J.B. "Cap" Harrelson, meet manager and referee, as well as a National Amateur Athletic Union official, along with 1948 Olympic shot put champion, Wilbur "Moose" Thompson. After Leon popped the metal ball out 60 feet ¼ inch, the throw was measured and remeasured. Officials carefully weighed Leon's implement: 12 pounds 1 ounce. The ring was measured and the ground was examined for any slope. All was perfect.

There was almost a second mark to submit. As Pete Gianopulos reported, "Later in the afternoon, the Wildcat weight man uncorked three discus throws in the neighborhood of 180 feet, but fouled on all of them." Nevertheless, his winning throw of 164 feet, 8¼ inches was a new meet record. It had been quite a day for the kid from Derby Acres, and that evening he ate his first steak. Reporting the meet in the April 21st edition of *The Bakersfield Californian*, Tom Liggett described Leon as "affable, unassuming, quiet" and revealed that he "plans to become a farmer." Liggett's story also disclosed that meet referee Harrelson intended to immediately submit to the national federation a formal application for recognition of Leon's record.

Three weeks later, May 11, 1952, the day after the prestigious West Coast Relays, the *Taft Midway Driller* reported, "Leon Patterson, Taft High's sensational young weight man, was credited with a new world's interscholastic record of 60 feet, 6½ inches in the 12-pound shot Saturday in Fresno, in Radcliffe Stadium, where he led the Wildcats to their first West Coast Relays title." Leon inspired Taft

High School's small team to a stunning championship before 15,000 fans, defeating powerhouse programs such as Alameda, Edison (Fresno), Bakersfield, and Washington (San Francisco) among many others. Leon also won not only the shot but also the discus (164 feet 10½ inches), while teammate Denny Cutland took the pole vault with 13 feet, Ted Switzler placed third in the high jump at 5 feet 10½ inches, and the sprint medley relay team of Elvin Urquhart, Gary Mulford, Bill Knick, and Jerry Wooliver placed third. That was the greatest team victory by Taft High School in its track and field history. On top of that, Leon was presented with a trophy as the meet's outstanding high school athlete.

Before the road trip to Fresno for the West Coast Relays, Dolores O'Brien had bought Leon a Hawaiian shirt, and she said, "He was thrilled...couldn't get over the shirt." Dixie added that it became his favorite. Meanwhile, his season-long shot put battle with the Kansas strong boy, Bill Nieder, was being followed by track and field fans all over the nation, but especially in Kansas and California. Of course, Leon didn't limit himself to the throws in dual meets that season, but continued to run the sprint relay, the 100-yard dash and to broad jump; he had improved his bests in the latter two events to 10.2 seconds and 21 feet 6 inches, respectively, mostly accomplished with raw ability rather than much technique.

Later that month, at the Central Section "Masters Meet," the state semi-final, Leon again won the shot, this time with a put of 58 feet 6 inches — a new meet record but disappointing to him — and he swept the discus, too, with a record toss of 168 feet 1 inch. Coach O'Brien urged him not to try too hard, but to relax and remember his technique. The long throws would come.

Patterson demonstrated his competitiveness with his final high school performance at California's state championships in Los Angeles a week after the "Masters Meet." Nieder had by then surpassed Leon's pending national record on May 16th, tossing the 12-pound shot 60 feet 9½ inches at the Kansas State championship meet. On May 24th, Patterson not only triumphed and regained the national record with a 60 feet 9½ inches put, but in the process won what was then the finest high school shot put competition ever, with all five placers surpassing 55 feet. Runner-up Don Vick of Chaffey High School put the shot 59 feet 7¾ inches, which would have won every other state meet in the nation except Kansas.

Leon also took the nonscoring 16-pound shot put event with a record 49 feet 2 inches. He topped another unbeaten campaign, and led sportswriter John de la Vega to label him, "The superman from Taft High." After he regained the national record, Leon told reporters, "It didn't feel like a good put. It seemed to slip off my hand and it hurt my wrist." De la Vega's article didn't mention Leon's second gold medal, but it did reveal to the world what had previously only been a rumor to most: "Patterson, also a great fullback prospect, has a serious kidney ailment that some medics say may cut him down in his prime of life. But other specialists say his life expectancy can be normal if he holds down on physical exertions. Leon expects to go right on shot putting, 'tis said at SC, but his pigskin days are over."

That year, due to safety concerns, the discus was not contested in the California state meet. Too bad, because Patterson, with a best throw of 177 feet 5 inches, led all competitors nationally by over 10 feet in that event. By season's end, he had six times exceeded 60 feet in 12-pound shot put competition. Given the circumstances, he completed the finest season ever for a high school thrower, finishing it with his best-ever put of the shot despite having broken a small bone in his right wrist, so his hand and wrist had to be carefully taped. That injury would limit his shot putting as a collegiate.

There was to him an even darker cloud than his health that he could not escape: "It always bothered Leon that not once did his parents ever come to any of his high school track meets, not even when he won state championships," Dixie explained. He was by then no longer living at home.

Ever "one of the guys," Leon joined fellow jocks Gary Green, Elvie Dalton, and Elvin Urquhart on a drive south one weekend to The Pike, an amusement zone at Long Beach, where all got tattoos on their right biceps, a rebellious act indeed in those distant days. With most of the same group (not all participants have been identified), he later embarked on another adventure, driving farther south, all the way to Tijuana, in search of "Spanish Fly," the fabled compound that supposedly rendered girls sexually insatiable. Once there, remembered Urquhart, "We elected Leon to go with the money down a dark alley for the exchange because we knew the seller would not dare steal from Big Leon." Elvin concluded, "The joke, of course, was on us since the 'Fly' turned out to be nothing but sugar."

Senior Ditch Day found Leon with basketball star Don Zumbro and another classmate, Emory Kent. The three "waited until late afternoon" Zumbro reminisced, "and took my car to Bakersfield. We were looking for girls or excitement but found neither. We drove around awhile and finally returned to Taft and had dinner in some restaurant in Ford City. Sad but true!"

Dick Henning said he had by then been eased out of Leon's social circle because Dixie considered him a bad influence, and that she had been correct in that assumption. Leon did still occasionally practice his throwing techniques at old buddy Elvin Urquhart's house. The Urquharts were another family that welcomed Leon, and Elvin also revealed, "My little brother (five years younger) was always hanging around. He was in awe of Leon, and Leon was so good with him. He taught Derald the shot put and the discus throws."

In May when yearbooks were delivered, Dixie later reminisced, the campus was full of students inscribing one another's copies. "Leon took mine and on the whole page wrote something like this: "To a girl who makes my heart beat faster when I am near you, and I become empty when you're away. If you still feel the same way in one year from now, will you do me the honor of becoming my wife?" She sure would.

A few days later, when Leon's name was called at the graduation ceremony for the class of 1952, a huge ovation rocked the stadium where the event was held. Dixie reported, "When he walked across the stage the crowd went wild." He had finished in the upper half of his class academically — which may have been his greatest high-school accomplishment — and his unassuming ways had made him popular indeed. Unfortunately, his parents didn't attend the ceremony, but his other families — the Kenneys, the O'Briens, and the Urquharts — plus a load of friends and acquaintances, certainly did, as did his brother Calvin, who had all along encouraged Leon to continue his education. After the ceremony, Leon and Dixie skipped the all-night class party and instead "drove to Bakersfield, had a lovely dinner, and danced."

Also in June of that year, athletic boosters at Taft High School arranged a banquet to honor Leon and his accomplishments. It was greeted with overflow attendance and speeches both exalted and amusing, and more than a little joshing from Leon's buddies. He was presented with an expensive luggage set embossed with his initials – LOP — in gold, as well as a treasured Block "T" bedspread. He was also expected to make a speech, so Dixie helped him rehearse. "He was nervous," she later reported, "but did all right." He said in part, "I'd sure rather be putting the shot than talking like this." Once more his parents were absent; their grandson, Lee, much later observed, "They didn't know the significance of those things. They thought of sports as just kids' games." Dolores O'Brien reported, "They just didn't show up. That really hurt Leon, and he never got over it."

After the state meet, Leon had relaxed; the week-to-week battle with Nieder was over, and the stress of high expectations for everything he did was largely relieved. He was ready to take a break. He had, however. been entered in the National AAU Decathlon Championships being held once more in Tulare, and he didn't want to let his coaches down, although his heart wasn't in it. After nine events, Patterson dropped out, having amassed 5,053 points while reinjuring his wrist. His performance was much overshadowed by another 18-year-old named Milt Campbell from Plainfield, New Jersey. Future Olympic champion Campbell finished second to Bob Mathias with a remarkable 7,055 points. Given all that was going on in his life, Leon must have felt some sense of relief.

TWELVE

Once his obligations to his coaches had been fulfilled and his final high school competition was behind him, Leon could enjoy what promised to be one final period of youthful fun. He and Dixie took her father to professional wrestling matches at Strelich's Stadium in Bakersfield, where they saw Gorgeous George in action, along with other worthies such as Billy Varga, Enrique Torres, Brother Frank Jares, and Carlos Molina, the Mexican Jumping Bean. "Leon got a real kick out of my dad, who really let his hair down. He drank a beer, yelled and shouted, smoking a cigar...this was a father I had never seen." Dixie added that Leon had said, "I bet that's the best time he ever had." Dixie concluded that she thought Leon had been right.

On another memorable occasion that summer of 1952, Dixie drove her parents' car out to the country where Leon had a summer job clearing wood. The area was populated by many jackrabbits, ground squirrels and doves, and Leon had brought his father's rifle with him that day. He told Dixie, "See that rabbit over there. I bet I can get it for our dinner. He shot and missed," she remembered, "then handed the gun to me and I shot it." Leon cleaned the rabbit and they roasted it over a fire on a spit they made, but "When it was done, we felt so bad about the poor rabbit that we buried it with the skin." Dixie made a cross out of sticks and grass and placed it over the rabbit's grave. "That's the last thing I ever killed," she later admitted.

Although he understood that college was the logical next step up in his life, Leon didn't want to leave Dixie and his surrogate families or his many pals. They constituted the only real support system he had ever known, and he felt safe, or at least safer, with them. The journey to the University of Southern California would take him not only to a new place but to a new culture, and it was daunting. If only Dixie could go with him. But, of course, Dixie couldn't; she had one more year of high school in Taft to complete. As a result, Dixie also felt the pain of future separation, especially since he was ill, and they couldn't know how long they would have together. Hours passed, sometimes whole days, without thinking about his illness, but memory of it always returned.

The young couple clung to one another as best they could, made love as often as possible, and tried to stretch their time together. She later said, "Leon was everything a woman could hope for in a lover. He was sensitive, and he loved to hold me in his arms afterward." Many years later, she would observe of their time together: "It was a short life, but good while it lasted."

Opening ceremonies for the Summer Olympics that year were held on July 19th in Helsinki, Finland, and Leon, along with many others in Taft, was deeply interested in the track-and-field events. Nearby Tulare High School had produced two alumni who were competing for the USA: defending decathlon champion Bob Mathias as well as discus thrower Sim Iness. Both won gold medals, and their success buoyed

Leon's dreams of one day representing the United States in Olympic competition.

Meanwhile, some central California residents were spooked by real or imagined sightings of flying saucers, a few of which supposedly hovered over the Westside petroleum reserves. "They're after our oil," was heard around Taft and its environs, often by folks certain that "Commie" agents piloted the disks. For a few moments on July 21, 1952, those people thought a Commie attack had come when they were awakened just before 5 a.m. by what turned out to be the most intense earthquake in the contiguous United States since the San Francisco devastation of 1906. Some locals still refer to 1952 as "Earthquake Summer," since the quake, which claimed 12 lives, was reportedly felt over 160,000 square miles, causing property damage estimated at $60 million, according to the U.S. Geological Survey. It was rated at between 7.3 and 7.6 on the Richter scale.

Taft was not unscathed, and aside from tiles shaken loose and sidewalks cracked, it even "led to a change in the oil production rate in Kern County," explained petroleum geologist Mohammed M. Masoumi. For instance, of two neighboring wells, one had 14 barrels a day increase in oil production, while the other had 48 barrels a day reduction, "different effects due to the natural earthquake." Workers didn't have to be forced to wear their hard hats that summer.

Dick Henning remembered an amusing aspect of the quake. In those days without much air-conditioning, "In the summer it was not unusual to suffer from 100-plus degree heat and, at night, we would wet the sheets, jump in bed and hope they would not dry before we went to sleep. Many people slept naked." The July 21st earthquake hit at 5 a.m., and "it was said that on that early morning, many neighbors saw each other in the buff in front of their houses. A story circulated that a woman screamed to her husband, 'Clarence, get back in the house; you don't have any clothes on!' He ran back into the house and there was another tremor. He came running out still naked but with his hat on."

A little over a month later, on August 22nd, a 5.8 aftershock killed two more people, injured 35, and did over $10 million more in property damage especially in nearby Bakersfield where old buildings had been weakened by the earlier shake. At least 20 other aftershocks of 5.0 or greater magnitude were felt, as were 188 of 4.0 or more. All over Kern County, people like the Pattersons and the Kenneys moved their mattresses outdoors and slept — presumably not naked — in their yards or in tents erected on their property. Others agreed with Lonnie Bundy, who said, "We're a-headin' back to Oklahoma! At least you can see a tornado comin'!"

Leaving his home town for the fall 1952 semester at the University of Southern California proved to be far more difficult than Leon had imagined it could be. While there is no record of his parents' response, it seems certain that his mother, in particular, missed him, but just as certainly the Patterson family could offer little material support for their son. Most of all, his emotions all but stopped him from leaving Dixie.

Leon was in a real sense departing for a new world. The University of Southern California was not just an athletic powerhouse, it was a culture within itself, an expensive private university with powerful alumni and a star-studded identity located in the vast and glitzy Southland. USC's athletes constituted a kind of aristocracy; to be a Trojan was to be a Golden Boy. Fortunately for Leon, Wildcat classmate Ray Herman, an outstanding football player, would be traveling with him, and the two high school teammates would be able to room together, thus adjusting together that first year.

In their blue jeans and T-shirts — still Leon's favorite costume — and with their small-town ways, both young men at first looked more than a little out of place. USC was certainly not the oilfields. Dick Bank, who then worked in the university's sports information office, said that during Leon's freshman year:

> When the track team traveled, the athletes were issued cardinal sports jackets and shirts with USC logos. You were supposed to supply your own slacks. Leon didn't have any slacks; he only had a pair of jeans. And no money. I remember it was a problem, one that embarrassed him, but I can't remember how it was resolved. Someone must have bought him a pair.

Photos from Leon's senior year in high school show him wearing what appear to be slacks, so he likely had at least one pair of which his Trojan acquaintances were unaware. Those new friends were certainly correct to assume that his wardrobe, like his wallet, was nearly empty. By then, of course, many families in Taft would have helped him financially if he'd asked, but Leon wasn't one to ask.

The University of Southern California nevertheless welcomed Leon Patterson. He was going to have to face academics without the help of Dixie, but the university provided athletes with tutors, and Leon took full advantage of that. He also was paid $75 per month as a part-time groundskeeper: "All the athletes on a full ride had what was called O and M (Operations and Maintenance) jobs," Dave Hollingsworth explained; " The most desired job was to have a 'spot' that you personally had to keep in good shape, grass cut, watered, leaves raked, no debris, etc. If you didn't have a spot you had to go to the office and get assigned a daily job, which could be anything." Leon had a spot, and Dixie recalled, "This usually meant keeping up his discus ring, which he would have done anyway."

Hollingsworth also revealed that "Leon had negotiated a clothing allowance that he suggested I get as he had done, but I never did." Many years later, Dixie further divulged that "Leon had a sponsor who gave him $75 a month." The "sponsor" was the owner of an appliance store in Pasadena, and she remembered having been invited to dinner at the sponsor's beautiful home. "Leon was nervous because he wasn't used to eating out in nice places," she said. "I told him just to watch me if he didn't know what fork to use, and just relax and enjoy the dinner."

Leon and Ray Herman enjoyed an unexpected treat when Elvin Urquhart's older sister, Meredith, a nursing student at Santa Barbara, was assigned to a tuberculosis hospital in the Los Angeles area. She telephoned the two freshmen at USC and told them she had a pair of extra tickets to the Ice Capades, and invited them to join her. For Ray and Leon it was a dazzling introduction to live entertainment, and one more wonder of Southern California. That first year, Leon began weight lifting, his program modified due to his fragile health. As Bank explained, "It was common knowledge when Patterson came to SC that he had some kind of kidney problem, that it was the reason he wouldn't play football." He added, "But no one I knew was ever aware he was dying."

The other freshman recruits for the track and field team included pole vaulter Dwight Chambers from Phoenix, miler Fernando Ledesma from Compton, and future football/ track stars broad jumper Jon Arnett from Los Angeles, and hurdler Jim Decker from San Pedro. All, like Leon, had been elite high school athletes, and the latter two would also be outstanding Trojan football players. Of the five frosh, only Leon was a small-town boy, and he absorbed some good-natured joshing. Another ex-Trojan, pole vaulter Ron Morris, said Leon had some rough edges, so, "We teased him a lot; 'You're in the big city now, Leon.'" Sprinter Rod Wilger admitted, "We ragged everyone about something," but Leon was "a man's man." Said team manager Jack Larsen, who became perhaps Leon's best USC friend, "He was a sweet guy on a person-to-person level." His teammates to a man reported that they liked Leon a lot.

Meanwhile, enough Americans that fall "liked Ike" to elect Republican Dwight David Eisenhower president of the

United States, an occurrence greeted with joy in much of Kern County. The President-elect soon fulfilled a campaign promise by flying to Korea, leading to speculation that the "police action" there might at last be resolved.

Dixie, meanwhile, was told of what may have been a hoax by Leon's teasing teammates. He reported to his girlfriend that some of his roommates "brought a homosexual to their place." All but Leon took turns going into a private room with him. "He thought it very strange that they would want a man instead of a woman," she reported. Shortly thereafter, Leon agreed to pose in a bathing suit for an art student, but "he was a little nervous after the homosexual incident. I told him if [the artist] bothered him, just leave, but he grinned and said, 'After I deck him.'" For Leon, Los Angeles was a strange new world indeed.

Even shot putting techniques, then in the midst of a revolutionary change due to the innovations of Trojan star Parry O'Brien, were strange to the freshman. O'Brien had introduced a throwing style in which the putter faced the back of the ring, crouched low, then exploded across it using a half-turn of his body plus the drive of his legs to propel the shot. This more efficiently employed the thrower's power as well as his speed. Leon was still using an older, upright position in which the putter's off-shoulder faced the front of the ring.

During the fall of 1952, Leon had done a little experimentation with Parry O'Brien's new shot put technique, which would soon revolutionize the event, but had decided to stick with the form Tom O'Brien had earlier taught him. His season best in the 16-pound shot was 51 feet 8½ inches, with five other performances of more than 50 feet. The scholastic record holder wasn't big enough to put the 16-pound shot, opined world-record-holder and Olympic champion O'Brien, who was a dedicated weight lifter. "He [Patterson] was good in the 12-pound. He used old technique, hadn't switched over to my form. I'd been at it only a year. It took three years before it caught on to where coaches could teach it." Leon's old wrist injury also made putting the 16-pound shot difficult.

His wrist had not healed well, so he increasingly turned his major interest to the discus throw where speed mattered more than strength and, Dick Bank noted, "Leon had small hands, stubby fingers, and threw the rubber discus rather than the one with a metal rim." The weight-training regimen he had initiated since arriving at USC added muscle to his frame, and he would eventually stand six feet tall and weigh a compact 200 to 205 pounds. At one point, he reportedly grew to the 220-pound range, but he soon dropped the extra poundage in order to retain his quickness in the ring.

USC teammate, Olympic discus champion and world-record holder (190 feet ¾ inch) Sim Iness, was one of Leon's heroes. Like Leon, Sim was a Central Valley boy and a Depression migrant. When Leon realized that he was Sim's teammate, he was at first flustered, but the cordial Iness later said, "We got along well. We talked about the Olympics... both Valley boys." Oklahoma native Iness added, they had both "gone through hard times." Sim would become a guru for Patterson, a special friend and mentor.

For the 1953 season, Leon focused on becoming the best collegiate discus thrower in America. The USC freshman pointed his long-term efforts toward making the 1956 Olympic team. Iness said of him: "One lone memory: his dedication, hard work, over-achiever. He wasn't big but powerful, great natural strength...reminded me of Fortune Gordien, about the same size." No small praise, since multiple national champion Gordien would that season set a world record of 194 feet 6 inches.

In those years college freshmen didn't compete on NCAA varsity teams, so USC had only a small, if select, freshman squad in 1953. In dual meets against rivals such as Occidental or UCLA or various junior colleges, Leon was up to his high school habit of entering multiple events.

Jack Larsen said, "When he'd win four or five events in frosh meets, there was decathlon talk." Against a strong junior college team from Los Angeles Valley College in his collegiate debut, for instance, he won the shot put and discus, and tied for first in the high jump. In April, against dual-meet rival the Occidental College frosh, a small school with a big track and field tradition, the "Trobabes" were upset 67-64. Patterson, however, ended up the afternoon's high point man, winning the shot put with a best of 50 feet 6 inches (despite his continuing wrist problems) and the high jump, then taking second in the javelin and discus. throwing 140 feet ½ inch to Jim Mathias's 141 feet 1¾ inches. Two weeks after the meet with Oxy, Leon put the shot 50 feet 8½ inches and threw the discus 151 feet 8¾ inches in a three-way meet against San Bernardino Junior College and Santa Ana Junior College. Mid-May at Modesto's California Relays, Leon won the junior college-freshman division discus with 150 feet 10⅝ inches and placed second in the shot put with 48 feet 3 inches.

Despite remaining competitive in the shot, Leon increasingly concentrated on the discus throw as his primary event. That injured wrist wouldn't seem to heal. Just when he thought it had recovered, he seemed to again tweak it while putting. Meanwhile, his best official discus toss that season was 166 feet 11⅜ inches, at that time the second best official throw ever for a college freshman. Leon's pal, Trojan football standout Bill Boswell, said of him that he had developed the "quickest release of any discus thrower ever...quick, explosive." Leon also dropped his time for the 100-yard dash to 10.1 seconds, high jumped 5 feet 11 inches, and broad jumped 22 feet.

Rumors about Leon's ill health continued to circulate, and *Los Angeles Examiner* sportswriter Melvin Durslag talked with the freshman and "asked him frankly how a guy felt when first informed he will live only until 25." With remarkable candor, Leon replied:

It was a pretty grim prospect at first. I had read about things like this happening to other people, but couldn't even start to believe it could happen to me. The thought of it made me cold and clammy all over.

The funny thing is that physically I had never felt better in my life. That's what made it all seem to completely unreal.

Soon I began to settle into stride, and now I take the only attitude you can. I say the hell with it. I feel everything is going to be all right. In fact, I know it will.

Sportswriters, who often treated athletic contests as if they were matters crucial to human existence, suddenly had an ongoing story that dwarfed wins and losses. Could this kid "win" his battle for life?

Meanwhile, USC was having an effect on Leon. When he returned to Taft for visits, friends noted that he seemed somewhat changed. Still cordial, he nevertheless carried himself differently. He was the same Leon, but possibly the Trojan polo shirt he occasionally wore gave him the appearance of maturity and confidence. Not that he had become a dandy: Dick Bank recalled that at USC, "Leon always wore a white T-shirt and Levis."

Dixie, meanwhile, was busy completing her senior year at Taft High, working at her part-time job at McCauley's Market, still active in the Girls' Athletic Association at school, and in the Senior Mariner Scouts. "I didn't have much time," she explained, "so when Leon came home on the weekends, I couldn't help him with his homework too much."

Perhaps he didn't need help since, with characteristic candor, he shocked her one weekend when home from USC by revealing that "he had paid a boy down there to take his tests for him. The guy would ask him how many he wanted him to miss and go take the test. Leon said all the athletes did it." That unverified claim troubled her.

On another of his many visits home during his freshman year, the young couple went camping at Morro Bay with her parents. "We slept out under the stars in separate cots, and walked along the beach collecting driftwood and shells." It was common for Central Valley residents to relocate to coastal communities when they retired, and late one evening, while her parents were visiting old neighbors in nearby Cayucos, Dixie and Leon "walked way down the beach in the moonlight and made love in the sand dunes. It was beautiful and it was hard to leave and go back to camp."

Because she remained arguably the best female athlete at Taft High, Leon liked to call Dixie "his Amazon," a nickname that tickled her because, as she explained, "He said he wanted to raise Amazon children, but I don't think he knew they were women because I was supposed to have only sons." Dixie, too, had been awarded a Block "T" blanket and was formally designated the Girls' Athletic Association's top athlete.

The high point of Leon's freshman season at USC came in May, when Dixie convinced Lillie Patterson to attend the 1953 West Coast Relays with her. It would be the only time Mrs. Patterson would ever see her youngest son compete. Leon, who had excelled in the high school division of the meet the previous two years, was already a fan favorite in Fresno and, according to the *Taft Midway Driller*, "received a tremendous ovation from fans" when he threw the discus a seasonal best to finish second behind world record holder Fortune Gordien in the open-intercollegiate competition, one place ahead of his hero and friend, Sim Iness. Leon's frosh marks were, in fact, ahead of the freshman accomplishments of Gordien and Iness, as well as those of fellow Trojans Des Koch and Parry O'Brien. With normal progression, he seemed to be a strong candidate indeed for the 1956 American Olympic team.

Thirteen

The Korean War ended on July 27, 1953, with an armistice rather than a victory for either side. America lost 25,604 combatants, with another 103,051 wounded, and 7,955 missing. In fact, neither side won, but both seemed to have lost. In Taft, boys began to return home as men, sometimes as damaged men, and more than a few enrolled at the local junior college where they tried to begin rebuilding their lives. Almost unnoticed by most adults that year was the appearance on jukeboxes from USC to Taft and beyond of "Crazy, Man, Crazy" by Bill Haley and the Comets, the first rock 'n' roll number to climb onto the pop music charts. More would follow.

Meanwhile, on Wednesday, May 27, 1953, the *Taft Midway Driller* confirmed the worst-kept secret in town when the "Women" section on page 2 was headlined: "DIXIE JO ANN KENNY [sic] TO WED LEON PATTERSON." It featured a beautiful portrait of the raven-haired Dixie and announced that rites were planned for the Methodist Church on the evening of June 20th. The stilted language employed by society writers of the time referred to Leon as "the benedict-elect,...an outstanding member of the 1953 Frosh track team" at USC.

Leon was in any case an impecunious "benedict-elect," so Dixie, who still worked part-time six days a week at McCauley's Market, bought their wedding rings. She earned a generous $1.25 an hour at McCauley's and felt as though the owners treated her like family. While employed there, she also became a minor hero when a woman parked her car in front of the store and left her child in it. Dixie, working at the front counter, noticed the car begin to roll, and she sprinted out, leaped into the driver's seat, and applied the brakes before a collision could occur. The youngster had accidentally released the car's emergency brake, and the mother had absent-mindedly left the transmission in neutral. In any case, serious consequences were avoided.

There was a prewedding complication, since the bride needed to have four impacted wisdom teeth removed before the ceremony. "I was badly bruised and swollen when Leon came to visit, and he could hardly look at me and stayed only a moment." She later suggested that "Leon reacted to illness in a strange way. It may have been because he was so ill."

Once Dixie had recovered, Taft's social event of the summer of 1953 followed on June 20th: the wedding of Dixie Joanne Kenney to Leon Patterson. Over 150 guests attended and both Bakersfield and Los Angeles newspapers covered it, but it was biggest news in the *Taft Midway Driller:* "A wedding of more than local interest was solemnized in the First Methodist Church June 20th as Leon Patterson, one of the finest athletes ever to attend Taft Union High School, claimed Dixie Jo Ann [sic] Kenney as his bride." Leon surprised some when he asked his coach and surrogate father, Tom O'Brien, to serve as best man, while two of his younger buddies, Elvie Dalton and Gary Green, were groomsmen. Dixie's maid of honor was her older sister Patricia — Mrs. Dick Dykes — while bridesmaids were close friends Gail McCabe and Jeanine Garrison. Dixie's young nieces, Richelle and Suzanne Dykes, were flower girls.

Dixie had used her savings to put a down payment on a 1953 black Pontiac Catalina hardtop as a wedding gift to Leon. When he received the car, Leon asked her, "Are you sure you won't miss pushing a car?" and she replied, "Absolutely not!" The $99-per-month car payments would later become a difficult "push" for them, but at first the gift seemed nearly miraculous to him. "Everything I had went into the down payment for that car," the bride later admitted. She also conceded that the car payments turned out to be "a backbreaker for us."

Boys will be boys, and "Leon worried that his friends would soap windows and do all kinds of mischief to his car, so we hid it in the preacher's garage," Dixie said. That ruse worked, and by the time the celebration was ending, they snuck to their car and drove south. Dixie changed out of her wedding dress in the moving car because Leon didn't want to delay their getaway and accidentally invite a shivaree.

The newlyweds "stopped at Gorman on the ridge route" and found a motel. "That night," recalled Dixie, "I wore a white lace negligee over a white lace gown. Leon wore a white T-shirt and underwear." His unromantic outfit didn't dampen their ardor, and Dixie wrote, "After making love we fell asleep for the first time in each others' arms. During the night we both awoke at the same time and did it all over again."

The twosome had planned to visit Mexico on their honeymoon, "but got only to Mission Beach. Leon wanted to go home," Dixie explained. He visited his mother, then the couple borrowed camping gear from the Kenney family "and spent the rest of our honeymoon camping at Bass Lake."

When they returned from the honeymoon, Leon quickly found a seasonal job at the Kovacovich grape shed near Arvin loading produce into iced boxcars. It was busy, physical labor that required steady effort on a sun-baked deck, then into and out of iced boxcars — in and out, in and out — with breaks only when the shed ran out of produce or when inspectors stopped the loading due to low sugar content of a batch of grapes.

Gary Ogilvie, then a prominent athlete at Garces High School, worked that summer at the same shed. He recalls seeing Patterson bury a hatchet into the wooden wall of a boxcar, then do one-arm pull-ups on it with first one hand then the other. Concluded Ogilvie, "He was awesome."

Dixie and Leon rented long-term a motel room with a small kitchen in Greenfield near her work, and he commuted 10 miles to the packing shed. Since the motel was next to where Highway 99 climbed up or down the Grapevine Grade, she later recalled that they heard trucks gearing up or down all night. She also said that their room had an icebox, and she kept forgetting to empty the drain pan, so they had wet feet much of the time.

Dixie, who was only 17, had taken a job as a waitress in a cafe at Greenfield. She said that the cafe had a juke box that played popular hits such as Les Paul and Mary Ford's "Vaya Con Dios" and Rosemary Clooney's "Come On-A My House," tunes which she and Leon enjoyed, although he also still preferred country stars like Hank Williams and Lefty Frizzell. She also remembered that there had been 32 seats and 4 booths for her to serve; it kept her busy, but she was young and strong and enthusiastic. "I worked the lunch and dinner shifts by myself," she said.

Alcoholic beverages were served in the café — though not by underage Dixie — and, as she told it, one night:

> *Two drunks were giving me a bad time. One was particularly obnoxious, and just at that time Leon came in. The guy bothering me looked like a weasel. Leon didn't say anything, but came up behind him and stood with his hands on his hips. The other guy nudged his friend, and he looked behind him. Leon said, "You*

wouldn't be bothering my wife would you?" The guy just took money out of his wallet, put it on his bill, and staggered out with his friend.

He might have been drunk, but apparently he wasn't crazy.

Although she'd known him for over four years, Dixie had many more discoveries to make about her new husband as they settled in and got to know one another ever more intimately. "Leon said he had never had a salad until I married him," she reported. "He ate everything I fixed, but we didn't have much money, so they were economical meals. His favorite treats at drive-ins or cafes, she reported, were a hamburger size or a chili dog washed down by an Orange Julius. He also loved spaghetti, she added, and she introduced him to spumoni, which became a favorite. His was not champagne taste…fortunately, since theirs was not a champagne income.

But they were young and in love and, when summer ended and they traveled south for the fall term at USC, they found a $65-a-month apartment near campus until something opened up in the married student housing complex. Dixie was hired as a bookkeeper at USC, so part of their financial security was assured. She earned $180 a month and, with Leon's $150 income, they could make ends meet. Those $99-per-month car payments meant they ate many casseroles, and when on-campus housing was at last found for them at only $35-a-month, they quickly accepted it.

The Pattersons happily moved to the athletes' compound of married student housing on Exposition Boulevard, even though residents called it "Poverty Row." Each duplex there was a refurbished World War II Quonset hut. Their new neighbors included Mr. and Mrs. Sim Iness and Mr. and Mrs. Bill Boswell, and nearly everyone it seemed was in a similar situation, broke but determined. Occasional neighborhood parties might develop around a pot of spaghetti or of chili, and perhaps a gallon of cheap red wine or a bag full of bottled beer.

At home Leon had a sweet tooth, and "loved it when I made homemade candy," Dixie explained. "I made fudge, English toffee, peanut brittle, taffy, which I taught Leon to pull. The one he loved the best was divinity. He liked me to put cut-up walnuts and maraschino cherries in it. I sometimes had to hide them or there wouldn't be any left for friends." Leon was in some ways still a big kid, and she added, "He'd even burn his fingers trying to swipe a lick out of the bowl before I poured it onto the pan...while my back was turned." She added many years later, "I look back now and I realize that things I took for granted growing up were all new to Leon."

There were other surprises for him. Once they were settled at USC, Dixie said, "I made him an angelfood cake." It was another first for her husband, and while Dixie ate one piece, he consumed the rest of it, then asked for another (from scratch) the next night. She thought he would soon tire of them, so she made another and another and another...seven in seven nights, and he still asked for one more. "I told him there was no way I was going to make another. I may even have said, 'Go jump in a lake.'"

Also, when Dixie and Leon originally moved into married student housing at USC, her sister "gave us some of her old furniture and a 9-inch black and white TV," the latter a luxury to them. Dixie, the homemaker, immediately began the process of making the rather shabby apartment livable. "We had screens with plastic sprayed on instead of windows. There were many holes in the screens where the plastic was gone," she explained. She sewed curtains for the kitchen window and otherwise tried to make the apartment home. Noting her skill with needle and thread, Leon asked her to make him a shirt. They went to a fabric store, and he picked out the material. "It was wild," she said, "what we call a Hawaiian shirt today. He was proud of it and wore it often."

That first Christmas as a married couple, Leon again told Dixie he had never had a Christmas tree, "so I bought one for $1.80. He said I shouldn't have spent the money, and he wouldn't let me buy ornaments, so I made popcorn and cranberry strings, and ornaments, and cut foil stars from gum wrappers. I caught him looking at it many times and knew he was pleased."

Urban Southern California was certainly not Taft — and vice versa. Small-town girl Dixie admitted, "It was scary walking downtown in Los Angeles in those days, but I was never afraid with him by my side." Southern California offered many inexpensive attractions that the young couple could enjoy. As a jock, Leon could obtain tickets to USC's home contests from other athletes, and he and Dixie took advantage of that. Whatever else about him that was changing, Leon's tastes didn't gravitate toward high culture; for instance, he loved roller coasters, and after they had settled in Los Angeles, he took his wife to Long Beach to ride one — not her favorite activity, as it turned out. He took her, as well, to the Mr. Los Angeles competition, which she described as a "muscle show," and he also took her to her first strip show. She later described one ingenue with boobs so big they looked like "small watermelons...what an eye-opener!"

Dixie also remembered an example of how their small-town gullibility could be taken advantage of. "One time we went to a place that was like a flea market is today," she later reported. "We were standing around and to my horror Leon bid on a fox coat for $10." Dixie didn't care much for it and didn't want to have to wear it, but when they tried to pick it up, the salesman talked Leon into purchasing a more expensive pelt. "Leon liked me in a marmot coat and, try as I would I couldn't talk him out of it. $75 — our rent money." She knew they had been scammed, but he was happy with the purchase. As seemed nearly always to be the case, his heart was in the right place, but his judgment needed maturing.

Youthful inexperience showed in other aspects of the couple's life, such as when an insurance agent tried to sell them a policy. Leon was interested but Dixie — knowing he couldn't pass a physical examination — told him they didn't need it. Then the agent said that no physical was required, and Dixie said, "Maybe we should consider it. When I changed my mind Leon changed his and no longer wanted the policy he had been all for before."

Leon and Dixie were perhaps the youngest couple in married student housing. They were also well aware of their own lack of sophistication or of much social experience. Dixie recollected being invited to a party at the residence of Sim Iness and his wife, "but Leon and I felt we didn't really fit in" because most guests were older. When Leon and Dixie returned to Taft, though, "everyone knew us and would wave, say hello or stop to talk. Afterward Leon would look at me and I at him and say, 'Who was that?'" The young couple's attire was undergoing revision: She was now an office worker at USC, not a grocery clerk in Taft, so she dressed more like a young professional; he was a Trojan, part of a grand athletic and academic tradition, so jeans and a T-shirt were no longer his lone costume. Recalled old buddy Elvin Urquhart, "He looked like a million bucks."

Much to their surprise, Leon and Dixie were visited unannounced in Los Angeles by Leon's parents, and his father brought his son the rifle with which Dixie had once killed a rabbit near Taft. She wasn't clear whether Mr. Patterson thought the city was so dangerous that the young couple needed to be armed, but she was certain "it was one of the only things he had ever given Leon," who "treasured it." For reasons she never understood, however, "Before Leon died, Marvin came and took the gun back."

Part of the couple's routine at USC, Dixie later recalled, even as his health slowly failed, were practice sessions at the track and field facility. Leon never gave up trying to improve his throwing technique, and teammates reported seeing the blond athlete and his ebony-haired wife walking hand-in-hand to the practice discus ring on long, warm Los

Angeles afternoons and evenings. When Leon worked on his throwing form off-season, Dixie often "shagged" the discus and tossed it back. She had been performing that service for several years — high school and college — and the athletic young woman had become a pretty fair discus thrower herself, accepting pointers on style from her husband. By then, though, she was far more interested in being a wife and perhaps a mother, so she resisted the temptation to become competitive.

Fourteen

Upon returning to USC in the fall of 1953, Dixie and Leon soon settled into a domestic routine and did their best to put his health out of their minds. On evenings, after returning home from work or class, they'd eat, do dishes together, often toil over his class assignments or perhaps wander to the nearby field where he'd take a few extra practice throws, then they'd either watch their tiny television set or play games like Monopoly or Aggravation. "Leon was proud that I was a good cook and often I would have a surprise friend of his to cook for when I got home," his wife recalled, then added, "He never let me know ahead of time." Occasionally, after dinner, they'd walk on campus or visit neighbors, mostly fellow athletes and their families.

Dixie's pregnancy came as a surprise to both of them since, as she explained, "I've never been regular." About the time fall semester opened, she began to feel quite ill; "I thought I had the flu." She "could barely stumble from the bed to bathroom to throw up," and "couldn't keep anything down; so I tried to drink water so I would have something to throw up. When I was so weak that I stayed on the bathroom floor," she continued, "I guess Leon finally realized I wasn't faking it. He got something from a doctor, and I took it and started doing better."

When her physician at last announced that she was pregnant, he then tried both an injection and pills to stabilize her nausea, but "nothing worked. I threw up for four and a half months, and then was fine." Once Leon realized what was happening, he "was happy I was pregnant." Her husband, she added, "would bring me soda crackers in bed before I got up, but it didn't work."

Dixie was happy to be expecting, despite that period of severe morning sickness. Her husband's immaturity showed in both his insistence that his wife must deliver a boy as had his own mother, and his desire that Dixie give birth at home because his mother had. "I reminded him that he had almost died when he was born, and that a hospital was much safer for the baby," Dixie said. She added, "I had still some bonds saved from working when I was younger, so was able to pay for it."

Leon also wasn't "knowledgeable about what a pregnant woman should and should not do," his wife reported. "When I told him I shouldn't lift one end of the heavy couch we had, he got angry at me. He said I always could before," she added. "He also insisted on my painting our living room when I was pregnant. I told him the paint fumes sometimes caused you to lose the baby. He said he'd never heard of anything so silly." As it turned out, there was a great deal he'd never heard of.

USC then had a rule that women employees could work only for the first six months of pregnancy. Fortunately for the Pattersons, who needed her salary, a series of absences by fellow workers allowed Dixie to continue at her job for nearly eight months. That was fine with Dixie, who felt able to work and whose pay kept them above water.

As the 1954 track season approached that spring, the USC Trojans appeared to be formidable enough to claim yet another national collegiate championship. A headline in the *Los Angeles Times* seemed to say it all: "Trojan Spikers Loaded Despite Loss of Stars." In the short and long sprints alone, they would be represented by Joe Graffio, Howard Bugbee, Rod Wilger, Mike Larrabee, and Jim Lea — all national-class athletes; Jon Arnett in the broad jump, Wally Levack in the pole vault, and Willard Wright in the high hurdles also appeared to be solid; Ernie Shelton and Jack Findley in the high jump as well as Des Koch and Leon in the discus were strong medal contenders, and so on.

But both Leon and Dixie were by then aware that he had lost consistency as a discus thrower. During off-season practices, he might flutter the platter out in the 140-foot range for a couple of throws, then pop one over 160 feet on his next effort. His footwork was ragged because his feet were often swollen and sometimes all or partly numb, so his noteworthy speed in the discus ring was inhibited. More than once he fell, a rude awakening for one with coordination as fine as his. At other times sensations in his fingers were reduced and the platter would slip from his hand. Nevertheless, with Dixie's encouragement, he determined to work through such difficulties. His goal remained to throw over 200 feet and to make the 1956 Olympic team. If hard work could accomplish those things, then he would accomplish them.

Once team workouts officially began, Leon found a formidable rival in teammate Des Koch, one of those football-track athletes that USC coach Mortensen loved. A little over a year older than Leon, Des had not competed for the track team the previous year, but he had been one of the nation's premier punters on the football team. Des was about Leon's size — 6-feet 200 pounds and was, like Leon, fast and highly competitive. Unlike Leon, however, he was healthy. Sprinter Rod Wilger recalled that "Des was quite close with Leon, worked closely with him." Koch entered the 1954 season with an official best discus heave of 166 feet 3 inches, only inches behind Patterson's 166 feet 11⅜ inches. By midseason Des had bests of 177 feet 5½ inches in the discus, 52 feet in the shot put, and 213 feet in the javelin, making him America's leading all-around collegiate thrower.

Another of Leon's new teammates in 1953-54 was freshman pole vaulter Ron Morris, like Leon a national interscholastic record holder and a great natural athlete. Morris would in 1960 win an Olympic silver medal. The two young men hit it off right away, and Morris, a Glendale native, had great fun teasing Leon about being a hick from Derby Acres; he found that the good-natured weight man gave as well as he took. Morris also noted, "The guy was a super athlete. I had the feeling he was destined to be a world-record holder."

Both Ron and Leon, like most world-class athletes, were extremely competitive as well as physically gifted, and Morris said they had contests such as how far they could throw a discus while doing a one-armed handstand, or how far they could long jump backwards, or how far they could walk on their hands before dropping. Not Olympic events, of course, but great fun for those gifted athletes.

Ron also reported that Leon was close to his teammates who, according to sprinter Rod Wilger, "ragged everyone about something." Wilger added, "Leon was in the class with other guys at school expected to score big in the nationals. I remember basically the way he thought, the way he acted, The coaches expected him to be a future championship athlete for USC. He carried himself like he expected to be, too." Added Morris, "Patterson was very quick, with excellent technique...so powerful within that smaller frame. Watching him throw gave you the feeling of him having great strength under control."

Nevertheless, Leon was at times visibly not well during the track season of 1954. As a result, he remained less consistent, especially when he occasionally suffered from headaches, blurred vision or swollen extremities. He would some days return home from practice and crawl directly into bed. Parry O'Brien observed that Leon was "a very erratic performer, with 144 feet one meet, then 175 feet. Up and down. I attributed that at the time to his disease." As the season went on, Leon did indeed seem to slump, pep up, then slump again. His intensely competitive spirit caused him to try harder, but that resulted in tightness that could lead to more frustration.

In a dual meet against Occidental, for example, Koch won the discus with a throw of 163 feet 6 inches, while Patterson finished second with 158 feet 10 inches. At the annual AAU Relay Meet on March 13th, Leon tossed an even 170 feet, beating Parry O'Brien's 165 feet 6 inches but again losing to Koch, who threw 172 feet 11½ inches. Mid-April at Santa Barbara's Easter Relays, conditions were good and Koch finished second to Fortune Gordien with a personal best of 177 feet 5½ inches; Leon also managed a personal best of 175 feet 3 inches in fourth place, with O'Brien third. Four of America's five best throwers had competed there.

A multi-event competition on May 3rd in Pasadena, the Muir Pentathlon Meet, included a pair of special exhibition events: the two-handed shot put and the two-handed discus. Each competitor threw with his right hand then with his left, and the combined distance determined the winner. It was a relaxed, unofficial but high-quality competition. World-record holders Parry O'Brien in the shot and Gordien in the discus won the two-handed events. Not much noticed was that Patterson had managed the longest discus heave ever for a college sophomore, 178 feet 8 inches. That was a new personal best for him and the eighth best throw in the world that year. That Patterson achieved such a mark as a sick sophomore was put in perspective by Olympic champion Sim Iness when he pointed out, "I held the national junior college record at 164 feet. If Leon had been in junior college, he would have broken my record by 14 feet."

Trojan coach Jess Mortensen then announced to the media, "Leon Patterson is through with shot putting. He has a bone growth on his wrist from high school, but it doesn't bother him throwing the discus." Meanwhile, Leon and Des's banner season continued, and a *Los Angeles Times'* article in May began this way: "One of the hottest collegiate discus rivalries in history resumes this Saturday in the Coliseum when SC's Leon Patterson and Des Koch have at it again in the highlight of the SC-UCLA dual meet." It went on to say, "Jess Mortensen's two blond strong boys are the two top platter men in the country." That was confirmed when the NCAA released its list of best marks nationally for the season on May 8th: Leon Patterson of USC was first (178 feet 8 inches) and Des Koch of USC was second (177 feet 5½ inches).

Meanwhile, as the track season of 1954 moved into mid-May and continued heating up, it was not developing in a vacuum: Earl Warren, the Chief Justice of the United States Supreme Court and a graduate of Taft's long-time rival, Bakersfield High School, wrote the opinion in a decision known as Brown v. Board of Education. The ruling forever changed American society by declaring racial segregation in public schools unconstitutional. Citizens in nearly all-white Taft, and in *de facto* segregated Bakersfield, certainly took notice, and Warren became a hero to some, a villain to others. Few savvy people were indifferent to him. "Impeach Earl Warren!" signs appeared in his home county where old racist habits died hard.

Leon and Dixie, who by then had rubbed social elbows with athletes and students of all colors, simply went about their lives, but they were growing both socially and intellectually. As a high school boy, Leon had answered "farmer" or "work in the oil fields" when asked about his long-term ambition. By 1954, as his experiences continued to broaden, and as he came to understand what a university education might accomplish, he was more apt to reply when asked about his ambitions, "coach" or "teacher."

Throughout that track season, with all of Leon's ups and downs, Dixie's pregnancy was the Patterson family's major issue. Fortunately, as spring progressed her condition became less and less troublesome, which was a good thing, because the first few months had been so difficult. When her job at the university ended due to her pregnancy, Leon and the track team were on the road a good deal. Dixie's due date was June, so she arranged to return home and have her baby in Taft.

That wasn't easy for Leon, whose best friend and most intimate confidante, Dixie, would be for a time gone. June brought not only Dixie's due date but the year's biggest track meet, the National Collegiate Athletic Association Championships in Ann Arbor, Michigan. As her husband prepared to fly east for the nationals on June 10th, Dixie went into labor at her parents' house, with pains only 10 minutes apart. When she announced to her mother that contractions had begun, Mrs. Kenney "ran to the phone and called my sister. My sister ran every stop sign in town on the way to the hospital." Once Dixie arrived at Taft's Westside Hospital, she was given a saddle block that slowed down the frequency of the pains, but only four hours after starting the process, at 4:04 a.m., Dixie delivered a 7-pound 15-ounce son, whom she named Orel Leon Patterson, Jr. Despite the mother's dark hair, little Lee Patterson, like his father, was a blond.

Patricia Dykes, Dixie's sister, was then able to get a message to the plane carrying the Trojan team to Michigan before it took off, and it was announced over the intercom that Leon Patterson was now the father of a son. "I guess he was pretty happy," reflected Dixie in a triumph of understatement.

When Leon arrived in Ann Arbor:

He called me and I was able to walk to the nurse's station. He was really excited about Lee and wanted to know all about him. I told him that Lee was the prettiest baby I'd ever seen and wasn't red like most, but was white and beautiful. He said boys aren't beautiful, they are handsome. I said okay, he is the handsomest boy you've ever seen.

The father, delighted as he was, had been feeling ill indeed. He was suffering more and more often from "blurred vision, lower back pain, swollen feet and ankles, and headaches." Team manager Jack Larsen recalled, "I've never forgotten riding on the bus from a hotel in Ann Arbor to one of those 1954 NCAA meet sessions. I sat next to Leon. We got to talking about his feet and ankles. At that stage, he was having to cut his track shoes to get into them. He told me it was Bright's disease, and it hit home because my own dad died in 1938 of the same thing."

During the discus finals at Ann Arbor, Leon seemed to be enduring one of his bad days. He became frustrated at fluttering the discus to only the 150-foot range, or throws that sailed beyond the zone so weren't measured, while Jim Dillon of Auburn and Des Koch took the lead nearly 20 feet ahead of him. Jack Larsen remembered "Leon getting angry, and that was rare, for foul throws." The outcome looked grim, and as Dick Bank recalled, "Leon came from far back on his next-to-last or last throw and took third place at 169 feet 1 inch." Coverage in *Sports Illustrated* later opined, "Under the circumstances, it was immeasurably the most heroic performance of the meet if not the meet's history." Meanwhile, USC easily won the team title with 66 points, more than double the tallies of runners-up Illinois and California.

Dolores O'Brien observed that "Leon thrived in competition. Tom always admired that most about him. In the most important meets, he was at his best." His best at the NCAA meet that year officially certified Leon as an All-American athlete, but he couldn't wait to return home to meet his son.

"When Leon got home late one night, I was waiting up for him," Dixie later wrote. "He surprised me, when I opened the door and he pushed past me. He had to see his son first before hugging me." Once they returned home with their baby to their own quarters at married students' housing, Dixie said, "I would be cooking dinner and look around the door to find Leon playing with Lee on the floor where I had placed a blanket. He really loved him."

Leon had one more track and field commitment that season, the National AAU Championships in St. Louis. As happy as he was with his new son and with having officially become an All-American, he was drained by the demands of the season on his ailing body, and by the emotional roller coaster he'd been on as an athlete, as a husband, and as a new father. Nevertheless, he flew with teammates to St. Louis on June 17th. Given his condition, he threw surprisingly well – 165 feet 6 inches — for sixth place behind winner Fortune Gordien, but his heart wasn't in the effort. He was sick and he wanted to be home with his wife and their baby.

Fifteen

Following a short rest during which he bonded with his new son, Leon again worked at the grape packing shed near Arvin during the summer of 1954, and Dixie joined him when she could. With a new baby that summer, they needed all the income they could manage, and Leon in particular seemed driven. Little Lee was suffering from colic, vomiting nearly all he ingested, so Dixie experimented with various formulas, finally settling on the one he had tolerated while in the hospital. Meanwhile, the young father's sleep was fitful and his work days were long; it was not the best schedule for a sick man.

There was no laundromat near their temporary residence in Arvin, so the young mother had to wash cloth diapers (as well as their own clothes) in a sink. Between caring for her baby and worrying about her husband's increasingly swollen body, she too was often exhausted. "There was no recreation during this time...we were both tired at the end of our days." Leon seemed increasingly obsessed with providing some financial security for his family as his health continued failing, and when he learned that a woman was needed at the packing shed, he and Dixie arranged for a babysitter while she became a packer...one of the fastest in the shed, as it turned out, earning 75 cents an hour (Leon was paid a quarter more).

It was also not uncommon for some workers to fail to show up for their shifts, or for the delivery of produce fresh from the fields to both accelerate and continue into the night. As a result, long days were available to those strong enough to handle them. Leon put in many double and even triple shifts despite his gradually deteriorating condition. "We could work overtime as long as we wanted," said Dixie. That summer, she said, she could tell that her husband felt death closing in on him, as well as the responsibility of providing for his family. Beleaguered by the fear that he would leave Dixie and Lee with nothing but bills, he did the only thing he knew how to do, working longer and longer days in the unforgiving San Joaquin Valley heat.

"One day," she recounted, "after I had put in my eight-hour shift, Leon came and took my hand, saying their checker had quit and they had to get grapes packed into the railroad freight cars." She took the job and "kept getting more pay the longer I worked." As her salary bounced from time-and-a-half to double-time, she "earned the highest I ever had for one day, $25," which she noted was "a quarter of a car payment." When the couple at last returned home that evening, "We didn't even bother to take our clothes off but dropped into bed and fell fast asleep." On another night, the Pattersons were the last ones to leave the packing shed, and Leon grabbed his wife's waist and said, "'I want to see if you taste as good as those grapes!' We ended up making love on the packing shed floor," Dixie much later reminisced.

After the table grape season ended in Kern County, Leon and Dixie couldn't find work near home, so he insisted that they travel north to Mendocino County where he had toiled with his parents when he was a boy. They would pick peaches. The journey was particularly difficult for Dixie, since she had to leave her baby with her parents. Leon "promised to take me home every weekend to see him, but when we got up there we worked all the time, and I didn't get to see my son for six weeks," she later wrote.

She did get to experience first-hand the life Leon had grown up with — hard work and camping with other pickers. But with their nearly new car and expensive camping equipment borrowed from Dixie's parents, the Pattersons stood out among workers. "The people in the campground were poor compared to Leon and me," she later wrote. The Pattersons had a camp stove and an ice chest, but "some of the other campers cooked over open fires and had blankets on the ground for their beds. We had a metal camp bed with a mattress, sheets, pillows, and blankets." The young couple also had a tent, plus "a camp stove with a portable oven." Leon would occasionally return from work with his pockets full of peaches, so his wife would cook them peach cobbler. "He was like a little boy when it came to food," she observed. "I used to tell him he married me for my cooking, and he'd wink and say I wasn't so bad in bed either."

Nevertheless, they were living in a sad world that Dixie had never before experienced, and she found herself upset at her inability to do much to help her poverty-stricken fellow pickers. She also admitted that at first "I worried that our stuff would be stolen while we worked, but nothing ever was." She was learning the lesson so movingly expressed by Ma Joad in *The Grapes of Wrath:* "'I'm learnin' one thing good,' she said. 'Learnin' it all a time, ever' day. If you're in trouble or hurt or need — go to poor people. They're the only ones that'll help — the only ones.'"

Those images of the poverty she had observed remained with her throughout her life, such as "a woman with a baby.

She put two peach crates side by side, upside down, then threw a blanket over them...put her baby over them with another small blanket over it. She was picking peaches although she looked eight months pregnant. The women there looked older than their age. Children scampered up and down the ladders that parents set for them, picking with the rest." As for the work, "We started picking at first light," Dixie explained. "Leon and I wore coats because it was cold, but dressed in jeans and light shirts. By afternoon it was hot. Leon would be stripped to the waist and grinning. He'd say, 'How do you like a taste of my life?' I'd grin back and say it was a piece of cake."

In fact, the harsh reality of a picker's life especially struck Dixie when she saw an older woman fall from one of the 14-foot ladders used to reach the high branches of the fruit trees. That occurred on a still, cool morning, so she and Leon took their coats off and covered the injured picker until an ambulance arrived. A few days later Dixie was near the top of one of the ladders when its tongue began to slip in the soft earth beneath. She grabbed a branch and screamed for Leon, who dashed to her aid and reset the ladder under her just before the branch broke.

On another day while the couple was picking peaches, the labor contractor brought a truck loaded with watermelons that for some reason hadn't passed the agriculture department's inspection, and told his pickers to help themselves. "Leon and I loaded the trunk, back seat, and even under my feet and between them with watermelons. I had one on my lap. We had a wonderful time driving through the campground delivering the watermelons to all the kids and poor families."

A canal ran along the edge of the field where Dixie and Leon were picking. After work in the summer heat, they would change into their swim suits and soak in the swift, cool water. A rope had been rigged for the use of those not able to swim in the rapid current, and Leon would anchor himself with it and catch her as she drifted by. It seemed to be a blessing until Dixie emerged from the water one day and found a leech attached to her groin. That ended the swimming for her.

Before long the young wife came to suspect that the labor contractor was cheating them on the count of their piecework, so she informed Leon, who confronted him. After a fiery scene, Dixie and Leon quit and went to work for another contractor, a Filipino, who turned out to be a far more honest and compassionate boss. Due to Taft's nearly all-white population, Dixie had virtually no experience with nonwhites, and Leon had only a little due to his participation in athletics, so this was an educational experience for both of them. When the contractor learned that Dixie had just had a baby, he assigned her a single set (four trees) to pick and told her that he would pay her to tally other workers' boxes and to keep his records. "They were really good to Leon and me. The contractor invited us to his home for dinner."

Her new job gave Dixie a glimpse of what she called a "sad part of pickers' lives. I made out the checks which the contractor signed. Some women tried to get there before their husbands, and when they found out they were too late their faces fell. I knew it meant a week of no food for them and their children" because the men tended to drink up their wages. The middle-class girl from Taft was growing up quickly as she observed the systemic poverty that undergirded California's agricultural affluence.

In evenings after dinner, Dixie and Leon would sit next to their campfire and listen to another extravagance that she had previously taken for granted, her portable radio. "When we got a day off once, we went to a drive-in movie," and her ticket stub was selected in a drawing for free passes to the theater. Since she and Leon would soon be leaving for Los Angeles, "I picked the poorest looking family in camp and gave them the family tickets."

Leon was learning, meanwhile, about how to be part of a functioning family. When a couple of his buddies from Taft showed up at the camp, he was delighted to see them, and he got them jobs with the contractor. It didn't seem to dawn on him that Dixie would now have to feed three appetites like his own, and to do it on an old camp stove after having worked all day in the peaches herself. Moreover, she was also "not only cooking but packing lunches until I said 'enough,'" she later wrote. "From then on, we ate out."

While they were still picking peaches, on August 21, 1954, Leon celebrated his 21st birthday. The couple went to a bar located next to the campground, where he savored his first legal drink. "It was a Singapore Sling," his widow later reported, adding, "I had a coke while he enjoyed it" along with an Elvis song from the juke box. That would be his final birthday celebration.

Dixie's own 18th birthday, meanwhile, caused stress between Leon and her when he refused to register the new car in Dixie's name as well as his own, despite her having provided the entire down payment. He was still influenced by the rules he had learned at home, so he left it in his and his mother's names. Leon was uniformly remembered as a good guy, but his domestic ideas had been formed by his parents' dysfunctional relationship — the husband was the absolute boss; the wife, while loved, was subservient — and he was still early in the process of learning more enlightened perspectives when illness swept him away.

On the other hand, he had learned to be a good provider. He continued working 16- to 18-hour days, and "Late that summer, Leon's ankles got really swollen. He went to see another doctor," Dixie reported. "He came back and told me everything was okay. But without Leon knowing, I went to see the doctor, and he told me Leon had about six months to live. As it turned out, he was almost exactly right."

Leon did not share details of his health with his parents, either. He did try to stay in touch with his mother and brothers, especially Calvin, who by then lived near Taft, but he had little communication with his father, with whom he had never been close.

Sixteen

When Leon and Dixie returned to USC for the fall semester, his deteriorating condition became obvious to most of his teammates and pals. Jack Larsen said, "He came back for the fall and he seemed much bigger. Well, I figured out later he was bloated from the disease. I said, 'Leon, you look great, much bigger.' He looked at me, and said, 'Yeah, I worked hard this summer.'"

Dixie remembered that she and Leon would most afternoons walk to a field next to married students' housing while their infant son napped next door. Leon threw the discus there, and Dixie — dashing back and forth to check on Lee — would tell him if she saw anything wrong with his form. His throws were falling shorter, and he "was steadily getting physically worse," she explained. "It wasn't his technique." He often threw until darkness made it impossible to follow the flight of the platter. Noted sportswriter Jim Murray summarized Leon's situation: "His life — all of it that meant anything to him — was composed of Dixie, the baby, and track, and his hours on the field were the price he paid for all three."

Leon's wife also added that, "When we went back to school in September, Leon didn't think I had gotten my flat stomach back from having Lee, so every day until he went to the hospital, he made me do 99 situps, 99 pushups, 99 jumping jacks, etc., while he counted." He was a physical man, and he couldn't seem to understand that your body might betray you, although his own by then was visibly waning. "He used to have perfect coordination," said Dixie. "He used to laugh at me when I'd trip over something and tell me I was clumsy. I think the worst thing of all was watching him stumble around the apartment bumping into things and falling over stools, trying to play with his baby."

By then, Leon was increasingly and visibly unwell. "One night he crashed in the bathroom trying to urinate," recalled Dixie, "and hit his head on the bathtub. He was unconscious and his ankles were terribly swollen." Neighbor and fellow athlete Bill Boswell remembered what turned out to be "one of his last outings. My wife and I took him to a picnic in Long Beach. We had a good time, then at 2 p.m. his whole body ballooned up — pain everywhere." The suffering would cause Leon to become "very bitter with anyone, his wife, too." Still, when he felt up to it, Leon continued to attend class, to play with Lee, to fling the discus, doing all he could to keep life normal for as long as possible.

According to Dixie, the young couple refused to accept her husband's prognosis. "When Leon got so sick," she later wrote:

> He first went to the USC clinic. The doctor there took me in his office and told me there was no hope for Leon. The doctor in Arvin told me he had six months, while giving me peanut butter cookies and milk. When he was transferred to the Good Samaritan Hospital, the doctor there took me out of Leon's room and told me Leon was dying. They all seemed to agree on one thing, that

Leon would soon be dead. I still kept on hoping for a miracle and Leon did too. Things like that just didn't happen to people like us.

Meanwhile, Dick Bank recollected, "In the fall Leon had problems. His eyesight went first. He began to bump into things." Earl Gustkey elaborated, "In September, 1954, in a USC classroom, Leon Patterson began having stomach pains. Then objects in his vision began moving in circles. Then, as if someone had flicked a light switch, he went blind. His failing kidney was driving his blood pressure nearly off the scale, triggering his blindness."

Even so, Leon attended the USC-TCU football game to cheer for his fellow Trojans though he could not see the field. After the young athlete's vision failed completely, he sought help, and Bob McNeish, alumni field secretary at USC, took him to Good Hope Clinic. which was associated with the university. Dr. George C. Griffith, Professor of Medicine at USC, moved Leon to Good Samaritan Hospital in Los Angeles, where he was charged only $1 a day, and where at least his symptoms could be treated.

A steady list of teammates and other friends visited. A few old chums drove south all the way from Taft to see him. Occasionally, teammates or pals had to help nurses try to hold him down while doctors worked on him when he grew frantic over an inability to breathe; they immediately discovered that his illness had not yet robbed Leon of his prodigious strength.

An article at the time, by the noted sportswriter Harley Tinkham in the *Los Angeles Mirror* was headlined, "Trojan Discus Star in Battle to Save Sight." Tinkham reported: "Leon hopes to be out of the hospital in a couple of weeks. But he must continue to rest and doesn't plan on returning to school and throwing the discus for another year. Dixie says she hopes to get a job to keep the family going." Still protecting the illusion that Leon's health problem could be cured, the young wife reportedly told Tinkham that she blamed "Leon's intense devotion to the discus and his overwork last summer for his present condition." Tinkham spoke for many when he concluded his piece, "Keep it up, Leon, we're all behind you."

When Dixie wasn't visiting Leon at the hospital, she tried to normalize her own life. "I had to keep busy, so I wouldn't have time to think. I just worked and planned for when Leon would come home." She "found a store discounting wallpaper and paint, then spent the time between hospital visits and taking care of Lee making our little apartment as pretty as I could." She made curtains, then sanded and painted the floor. Otherwise, she occupied herself tending to and playing with her baby. The busier she was, the less she thought about her husband's health. Nevertheless, gritty reality constantly imposed itself on the young couple.

"When I visited Leon in the hospital, the nurses were so sweet to me. They took Lee so I could have time alone with Leon," Dixie recalled. The stripping of his privacy and dignity was then especially galling to the young man, and his wife found herself acting as his intermediary. Leon's bed was surrounded by a curtain in the middle of a three-bed ward, and "If the timing was right he would have me help him with his BM on the bedpan. It embarrassed him to have the nurses do it." She added, "I always told the nurses how much and the coloring so they could chart it."

Leon was angry at his body, so he was not an ideal patient. While on a salt-free diet to help control his high blood pressure, for instance, he insisted that his wife sneak some beef jerky to him. When she refused, he told her to bring him some or don't come back. So she brought him a small pack.

He "insisted on coming home when I knew he shouldn't," his wife reported. "He did get to see all the painting and wallpapering I had done, but he was very ill." Dixie had to remain up all night with him "because when he laid down he couldn't breathe." Despite that, added

Dixie, "He was going to lick it, he said, but I could see he was dying." The life force was still strong in him, and he wanted to make love, but he couldn't so they settled for caresses. "The last night he was home with me," she also explained, "he made me promise that I would never marry again. I promised."

Finally, remembered Dixie, she talked him into returning to the hospital the next morning so "they could give him oxygen." Neighbor Bill Boswell drove the couple to Good Samaritan, while his own wife, Jo, cared for Lee. Leon was given a double room with one empty bed this time, and his wife found herself wondering if they'd done that to give him "privacy to die." She added, "When he was in the two-bed ward, he had a horrendous nose bleed. They had to pack his nose to stop it. He hated it," she added, "and wanted me to pull the packing out for him. I refused and he got real angry with me." In fact, his rage was directed against his own body that was failing him.

Leon also "kept asking for his mother, so I called and begged them to come, but they wouldn't. My sister and father, who I had called, went out and more or less made them come." Dixie was by then living at the hospital, sleeping in snippets on a waiting-room couch when she could. Her own mother cared for baby Lee at the university apartment. Leon had told Dixie that he hoped "if one good thing comes out of this, it's that my father quits drinking." Unfortunately, Dixie's mother later told her that all around the Pattersons' car in the hospital's parking lot "were beer cans. She picked them all up and put them in the trash." Leon's mother, meanwhile, suffered while watching what her youngest son was enduring. She had to leave the room many times to compose herself.

George Patterson received a call in Ohio, where he then lived, from his father telling him that Leon was "in the hospital and it looks bad." The older brother and his wife drove to Los Angeles so he could be with Leon, arriving on November 20th. "Leon was very aware of what was happening," George remembered. "He tried to make light of it, to joke. His body was badly swollen. His blood pressure was off the scale," the older brother reported.

Leon's teammate Sim Iness recollected, "I admired him so much for living the last year or so of his life with no hope; he was trying to get through one week at a time. The last time I saw him in the hospital he was yellow, bloated, kidneys just not working." Dick Bank added, "He was in awful pain when I went to the hospital, maybe a couple of days before he died. He thanked me for coming to see him, and he said it in a way that told me that he didn't expect to last much longer. I walked out of the hospital in tears. It was a shattering experience. To see the wife and baby there." Jack Larsen held Leon's hand the night before he died. "There were four or five of us in the room, and I said, 'Leon, what can I do?' He said, 'My lips are dry, can you get me some water?' So I wet a towel and put it on his lips. He was so bloated his eyes were swollen shut. It was brutal."

Dixie, meanwhile, had trouble accepting that things had turned so irretrievably wrong. "Sometimes I felt I was having a bad dream," she said, "and that I would surely wake up soon, but I just kept going one day at a time, hoping and praying for strength and guidance." She "asked a nurse what would have to happen before Leon could get better. She said 'diurese,' when his kidneys would start to work again by themselves, but it was one chance in a million." Dixie "prayed night and day for that to happen. When it did, I thought my prayers had been answered. The nurses and doctors were running in and out of Leon's room, and I asked the nurse what had happened. She told me his kidneys had started working."

Soon, he seemed to have stabilized. Relieved, the young mother at last returned to the apartment for the first time in several days in order to bathe, cuddle her baby, and catch up on much needed sleep. Meanwhile, her husband's remarkable body, which even then appeared formidable, continued to slowly kill itself. George Patterson, who stayed with Leon while Dixie was away, tried to share hope and offer comfort. "He really seemed to be feeling better," said George, "when he suddenly had a hemorrhage in his lungs and bled to death."

Dixie, meanwhile, was asleep at the apartment when her father awakened her and told her that Leon was asking for her. "I just knew then he was dead," she remembered. Her father, who hated Los Angeles traffic, drove her to the hospital. "When we reached the waiting room, Leon's mother blurted out that he was dead. I just sat down on the couch saying, 'My poor Leon. My poor Leon.' I was numb."

Leon Patterson's suffering had finally ended at approximately 3:00 a.m. on November 21, 1954. Dixie's suffering changed but didn't abate for a long, long time. She later wrote that she didn't remember how she got back to the apartment, but it was full of friends and relatives, and that she "just had to get out by myself, so I went outside and sat under a tree. The sun was shining, and I wondered how it could do that when Leon was dead." Bill and Jo Boswell joined her for that sad interlude.

Later, pole vault champion Ron Morris spoke for many of Leon's pals when he admitted, "...we were kids. What does a 21-year-old know about life? A lot of situations like that don't impact you until you're older, have maturity, but Leon's death was a trauma for me. A couple of times he was upbeat in the hospital, always talking about what to do when he was out of the hospital, but we knew he knew he wasn't going to make it."

George Patterson reflected, "I don't think any of us, including Leon, ever fully accepted that he was dying." Jack Larsen said, "After he was gone, I thought: He lived with this, the knowledge that he'd soon be gone. He knew what his life expectancy was. It was more than courage; it took a strength. I mean, he was a seemingly healthy young man and here was this disease, chopping away at him." Following Leon's remarkable come-through performance in the NCAA championship track meet that year in the face of worsening illness, Larsen reflected, "To me, that said more than anything about what kind of guy he was." And, of course, there were the "might have beens." How good might Leon have been if he hadn't been so ill during his two years at USC? Trojan teammate Ron Morris told Earl Gustkey that he had the feeling that "Leon was destined to be world record holder."

Despite knowing that Leon was terminally ill, others in the USC community, like some in the Taft community, including members of his own family, were stunned by his passing. So were many track and field fans nationwide. To local kids in his generation, he was and remains a tragic hero of almost classic dimensions, one who rose from poverty and was on the threshold of greater triumphs when he fell, fighting all the way. Coach Jess Mortensen, in the somewhat stiff but not insincere style of the time, told a reporter for the *Daily Trojan*, "He was one of the hardest working boys I've ever seen. He was an intense competitor who had his mind set on being a champion. He was a fine boy and extremely well liked by his teammates." Sportswriter Jim Murray eloquently summarized his memories of Leon this way: "He was one of the great athletes of his time; he was also one of the most dedicated, for to Leon Patterson athletics was the path of aspiration, of hope, of happiness."

Taft and the entire Westside became a community in mourning. People sought to do something — anything — to help the family, but many felt helpless in the face of Leon's passing. Ex-teammate Larry Peahl recalls that six days following Leon's death, the Taft Youth Center held a benefit dance for Dixie and Leon, Jr. "About 180 people came and donated generously," Peahl added. There was little else they could do.

Seventeen

One of Taft's largest funerals was held on November 26, 1954 — a frigid, windy day — at the same First Methodist Church where Dixie and Leon had been married on June 20, 1953. The list of pallbearers included Sim Iness, Parry O'Brien, Bill Boswell, Jack Larsen, Joseph Krunk, William Flood, Phil Bates, Dick Bank, and Elvie Dalton. Honorary pallbearers were Tom O'Brien, Jess Mortensen, Elvin Urquhart, Dick Dykes, Eugene Johnson, Maxwell Stiles, and Garland Basham. Composed mostly of Taft associates and USC friends, it was a glittering group, and none of them was happy to be burying this remarkable young man.

Following the church service, Leon's coffin was driven to the Westside District Cemetery on a low bluff just south of town. His husky friends carried it to the grave site and benediction was offered by the Rev. J. Alvin Crawford, who had so recently performed Leon and Dixie's wedding ceremony. *The Lord giveth — as in Leon's young family — and the Lord taketh away — as in his young life; it is not for us to understand.* More than a few friends lingered on the hill after the ceremony formally ended. From the graveyard, mourners could gaze to the northeast into the Great Valley, the heart of California, that had long before attracted the Patterson family and so many others. Some gazed west at rolling brown hills covered with oil derricks and pumps. Many admitted that they simply didn't understand, and many say they still don't. George Patterson later reported, "I consider myself blessed for having been his brother. Without a doubt. the world is worse off for having lost Leon with his winning personality and talents at such a young age." He added, "Leon's death crushed my parents."

For Dixie, a widow while still a teenager, everything had gone too fast to fully comprehend. "After Leon died, Tom O'Brien and another man with a truck came down to student housing and moved me back to Taft," she said. Having lost a surrogate son, for the rest of his life Tom could not see Dixie or Lee without weeping, the widow reported. Tom's relationship with Leon had grown much closer than coach-athlete, and consensus was that Leon's greatness as an athlete was the product of his own natural ability and determination, but also of Tom and Dolores O'Brien's unusually astute coaching and deep personal support. Lynne O'Brien Shelton fondly remembers, "As a young girl, I loved to watch my dad and Leon leave our house walking side by side to the high school, never saying a word, but talking the whole time. It was so fascinating, how could they *do* that?"

It took Dixie a long time to reenter life after her husband's passing. Part of her knew that she'd have to carry what she'd shared with him in a special chamber of her heart, and move on. Fortunately, she had Lee and her own kin to comfort her, as well as some members of Leon's family and many, many friends. A couple of times USC pals Dick Bank and Jack Larsen drove north from Los Angeles to take her to dinner and a movie. Old high school friends did what they could to help. Often Leon's widow "would bundle Lee up" and drive to the cemetery. "I knew that Leon wasn't there, but the shell that contained his life essence was," she reflected. "So I would cry and tell him how things were going and it was of some comfort. Lee slept comfortably on the seat of the car or I would hold him and tell Leon it wasn't all in vain; see what we created."

The December 6, 1954, issue of *Sports Illustrated* carried a touching tribute to Leon reportedly written by columnist Jim Murray of the *Los Angeles Times* (there was no byline). It said in part that "to Leon Patterson athletics was the path of aspiration, of hope, of happiness." It was also the path from his parents' rural Arkansas life to his own future in complex, post-war California.

In 1956, a schmaltzy, half-hour TV film about Leon's life starred John Erickson. More substantially, at USC the Trojan Track Alumni Award for the most inspirational freshman track and field athlete was designated the Leon Patterson Award. His hometown didn't forget Leon, either, and when the high school outdoor athletic stadium was refurbished, it was named Patterson/O'Brien Field. The Bob Elias Kern County Sports Hall of Fame in Bakersfield was opened in 1968, and Leon Patterson was an initial inductee (Tom O'Brien joined him there in 2006). Taft Union High School opened its own Hall of Fame in 2007, and two of the initial inductees were Leon Patterson and Tom O'Brien.

Wider recognition developed when *Los Angeles Times* sportswriter Earl Gustkey on April 30, 1991, paid Leon and Dixie a fitting tribute with a long, revealing feature story entitled, "Hard Life and a Short Life." It dispensed with sentimentality and revealed what the young athlete and his family had endured and accomplished. Much admired, Gustkey's piece was in-depth journalism of a high level indeed.

Back in 1954, Taft had remained for a long while a town in mourning. "There'd be times," admitted Elvin Urquhart, "when you'd run into some old teammate and for a second you'd just want to bawl." Following her own period of intense mourning, young and attractive Dixie Patterson began dating again because she knew she had to, and her swain was none other than Riley Jones, whom she had once dated during a hiatus in her high school relationship with Leon. This caused more than a little talk around town, and broke the romantic spell she and Leon still cast over some in Taft. But Dixie was by then a mother and a realist; she didn't want her parents stuck with the expense of supporting her while she raised her son. She married Jones in 1957, but the relationship, which produced another son, Larry Dean Jones, didn't last, and they divorced in 1962.

Only a year later, she married Jerry Wayne Nezat in Oklahoma City. The couple had been married for over 45 years at the time of the 73-year-old Dixie's passing in 2008, and they were the parents of one daughter, Mara Angela Nezat. In the early 1990s, Dixie demonstrated that she had never quite moved completely beyond Leon when she composed for her family a 130-page, handwritten personal history that detailed her version of the relationship with Leon, another life in another time.

Her son, Orel Leon Patterson, Jr. — Lee — is the father of three boys: Orel Leon Patterson III; Kenney Ernest Patterson, and Russell Eugene Hastings (whom Lee has informally adopted). Lee was an outstanding high school athlete while growing up in Estacada, Oregon, and he liked to recall that adjacent road signs near town tickled him and his family: "Cemetery Road" and "Dead End." Today he owns an automobile restoration business in his parents' home town, Taft. He also speaks fondly of both sets of his grandparents, and speculates that his mother had been "too negative" in her assessment of Marvin and Lillie Patterson. He also felt great fondness for Dixie's parents, Maurice and Minnie Kenney — "Grandpa was really funny" — and said he grew up loving to say Grandma's name, "Minnie Kenney."

Most of the older generation had passed away by the time of Dixie's death in 2008. Calvin Patterson succumbed in 1978; Maurice Kenney in 1975; Marvin Patterson in 1978; Lillie Patterson in 1982. Minnie Kenney survived until 1997. Coach Jess Mortensen died in 1962, and coach Monty Reedy died in 1994. Leon's old teammate and rival Des Koch lost his life in 1991, while his heroes Sim Iness and Bob Mathias succumbed in 1996 and 2006, respectively. All of those had mourned Leon in their private ways, and many had stayed in touch with one another as best they could: a community of grief. Said Chuck Werdel of Leon in 2012, "You simply don't forget someone like him." They were also all left to wonder what Leon and Dixie might have accomplished had they been granted a normal lifespan together. Might he have won an Olympic medal? Would his union with Dixie have produced other children? Could Leon indeed have followed the footsteps of O'Brien, Reedy, and Mortensen and become a coach?

Leon's surrogate parents, Tom and Dolores O'Brien, were devout Catholics, and they faithfully lit candles and had masses said for the repose of Leon's soul. In 1991, Earl Gustkey of the *Los Angeles Times* wrote, "Tom O'Brien is 78 now, ailing and frail. On nice days, he sometimes visits Leon's grave. Thirty-seven years later, he still cannot talk about Leon Patterson without crying." Tom died two years after that was written, and his widow lived for nearly another decade before passing away in 2002.

At the 60th reunion of Taft Union High School's class of 1952 in October of 2012, Leon Patterson was a presence. His son, Lee, brought a corkboard covered with clippings and photographs and other memorabilia, and many classmates laughed and occasionally suppressed tears as they discussed "Pat." One anonymous attendee snorted, "That guy was a stud horse!" as he blinked, then he walked quickly away. Elvin Urquhart, Leon's first close friend in Taft, grinned and said, "At least I could beat him in the hurdles...because he didn't practice the hurdles." Then he paused for a deep breath before he observed, "He was on the right track, Leon, and moving in the right direction. What happened to him wasn't fair and it still isn't. I'll never understand it." He spoke for many.

Talk in some cases drifted from the concrete hilarity of old games, old dates, old teachers — Mrs. Ihrig, Mrs. Baer, Mr. Newlee, and so on — to speculation about the meaning of it all. Why had they survived while Leon and other cherished classmates had died? Except for a few deeply religious alums, the explanation remained a mystery and more than a little daunting.

Dixie had by her own admission never quite understood what happened, either. Her 130-page handwritten and unpublished memoir closed this way:

When Leon died, I went to stay with my sister. One night I was sleeping on her couch when something woke me up. I couldn't see him, but I knew Leon was there. There was also a great presence. Leon spoke through my mind. He said, "I just came back to see my son one more time," so I walked into the bedroom and we looked down on Lee for some time. Then Leon was gone but the presence was still there. I went back to the couch and sat down. The presence stayed with me awhile longer and I knew everything would be alright. Then it left. I remember that with this presence there was a white light which surrounded us because I didn't have to turn on any lights to go to the crib. It left me with an extreme feeling of well-being. I knew I would make it somehow without Leon.

AFTERWORD

At the 1952 Kern Relays in Bakersfield, California, I was a 14-year-old freshman competing in my first important high school track and field meet. I stood nervously preparing for the finals of the "C" class 75-yard dash. "Come to your marks," called the starter, and with seven other boys I stepped forward, lowered myself to my knees, then pushed my spiked shoes against wooden blocks I had earlier secured in the ground.

As the starter called "Get set!" a murmur moved through the crowd but it wasn't for us. Across the field to our left, a husky young man wearing the blue and gold of Taft Union High School had entered the shot put circle.

Before the starter could fire his gun, the stadium erupted in cheers and applause, longer and louder than I'd ever heard, or so it seemed, and the starter called "Come up!" We sprinters stood, jogged a few yards, the returned to the blocks. I asked the runner in the next lane, "What happened?"

"Patterson, I'll bet," was all he said.

Taft Union High School's Leon Patterson had just become the first high school athlete to put the 12-pound shot over 60 feet in competition and I, kneeling in the starting blocks, had not seen it happen. Patterson was a high school senior when I was a freshman at Bakersfield's Garces Memorial High School; even though I competed in many of the same meets as he did, I knew him only from afar. He seemed to be the apotheosis of the many gifted athletes maturing in the San Joaquin Valley after World War II — Bob Mathias, Rafer Johnson, Ancel Robinson, Sim Iness, Leamon King, Lon Spurrier, and so on. The word among the young jocks was that Leon was a good guy, friendly with everyone, even "the colored boys" in those years of *de facto* racial segregation in much of California. More than a few of us yearned to be him.

Two-and-a-half years later, I was left stunned when I learned that Leon Patterson, All-American discus thrower for the University of Southern California, had died at 21. It didn't seem possible to us, his young peers. He had seemed to be a force of nature, preternaturally gifted, handsome, fortunate beyond our imagining. What had happened? How had nature gone so wrong?

I had recently played football against Taft in my senior season in 1954, and I was also a student journalist and a sports stringer for two commercial newspapers. I determined to learn more about what had occurred to this hero of mine, what beyond the vague "kidney disorder" reported in the local daily. Not knowing any better, I telephoned Taft Union High School and was connected to a sad but cooperative coach named Monty Reedy. He patiently responded to my naive queries. Later I spoke with Tom O'Brien, who indulgently answered my unsophisticated questions. Then I wrote what I still consider my finest piece of high school journalism, a commentary about Leon for my monthly column in *The Garcian*, my high school's newspaper.

I wrote about Leon again 37 years later, and by then I was a regular contributor to the *San Francisco Chronicle*'s Sunday magazine, *This World*. Preparing a remembrance of Leon, I spoke with Tom O'Brien's wife, Dolores, because Tom was recovering from a stroke and had trouble speaking. I spoke and corresponded with Dixie Nezat, Leon's widow, who struck me as being cordial, smart, and candid. So was their son, Lee. Then I wrote what I hoped was one of my better pieces, only to have it rejected by my editor as "too parochial." Fortunately, I was then also assembling a new collection of my own essays, *The Other California: The Great Central Valley in Life and Letters*, for Capra Press, so I included "Leon Patterson's Short Season" among them, and it was published.

Concurrent with my efforts, a journalist for the *Los Angeles Times*, Earl Gustkey, wrote that wonderful profile and summary of Leon Patterson's story, "Hard Life and a Short Life," that ran on April 30, 1991. I contacted Earl and learned that he was then contemplating composing a full-length biography of Leon, as well as a screenplay, since he had been contacted by movie interests. I much admired Gustkey's writing and was taken with his cordial demeanor, so offered him copies of my notes and correspondence with the Patterson family and friends. He reciprocated and sent me photocopies of his material. I also sent him a copy of *The Other California*. That, I thought, was that.

Promoting *The Other California* brought me in closer contact with Leon Patterson, Jr. — Lee — and his sons and a friendship flared. As others of my books were later published, I'd find myself promoting in Kern County, and Lee along with one or another of his boys would frequently visit Russo's Bookstore, my Bakersfield hangout. We spoke of many things, but never about the possibility of me writing a full-length biography of his father, even though neither Gustkey nor anyone else had ever published one.

Not until 2011, when my wife Jan and I completed work on *In Thought and Action: The Enigmatic Life of S.I. Hayakawa*, did I decide that I wanted to write another biography. Leon and Dixie's heartbreaking but courageous story seemed to me to be socially revealing and well worth telling. The next step was easy: In the hope that it would generate information about Leon Patterson, I wrote a brief piece on him that my friend Bob Price published in *The Bakersfield Californian*. It stimulated many responses, including an invitation to the 60th reunion of Taft Union High School's Class of 1952. Meanwhile, I found the 20-year-old notes that Earl Gustkey had sent me, as well as my own earlier notes, and Lee Patterson provided me with a copy of that remarkably candid, handwritten memoir his mother had written.

The die was cast.

Bibliographic Note

I encountered the Leon Patterson story as it unfolded in Kern County in the early 1950s. I was then a high school journalist and marginal athlete, who had not only competed in some of the same track and field meets as Leon, but who had also written about his death for my school newspaper in 1954. Many years later, at the end of the 1980s, two conversations — one with my writer friend, Bill Rintoul, and the other with an ex-teammate, Chuck Werdel — led me to contact Leon's widow and ex-coaches. I then wrote an essay, "Leon Patterson's Short Season," that I included in a 1990 collection of my nonfiction entitled *The Other California: The Great Central Valley in Life and Letters*.

This biography is an attempt to look more deeply into Leon's life and its meaning to those who knew him. The story's linchpin is an unpublished, handwritten memoir by his widow, Dixie Nezat, made available to me by his son, Leon "Lee" Patterson, Jr. Also of major importance has been a cornucopia of other material — notes, photographs, letters, memories — provided by Lee, as well as notes shared with me by Earl Gustkey of the *Los Angeles Times*; the latter included interviews logged with Ron Morris, Bill Boswell, Sim Iness, Dick Bank, Parry O'Brien, Rod Wilger, and Jack Larsen. Back issues of the *Taft Midway Driller*, the *Daily Trojan*, *The Bakersfield Californian*, and three Los Angeles newspapers, the *Mirror*, *Examiner* and *Times*, have also been important.

The recollections of Leon's high school pal Elvin Urquhart constituted yet another major source of material, as did the anecdotes and memories shared by Dr. Richard Henning, Milt Stark, Don Zumbro, Lawrence Peahl, Dr. Charles Hanna, Gary Ogilvie, Pete Gianopulos, David Hollingsworth, Charles Werdel, and Lynne O'Brien Shelton.

Among others interviewed, or corresponded with, or simply conversed with in connection with this book were:

Lonnie Bundy
Lester Carlson
Dr. John Collins
Jim Cox
Bill Dwyre
Judy Herman
Ray Herman
John Hillis
Pat Jamerson
Charles Kooken
T.H. Lockhart
Eddie Lopez

Neil McCabe
Dennis McCall
Frank McNeely
Marvin Mosconi
Ned Permenter
John Pryor
June Rieck
William Rintoul
Lynne O'Brien Shelton
Dick Snyder
Mike Stricker

Unfortunately, much of the published material referred to in this text is from scrapbooks and offers at best incomplete bibliographic information. Often dates and sources — sometimes even titles — were missing from newspaper clippings. Nevertheless, I felt competent to judge their veracity and employed those I thought important. In the list that follows, [PA] refers to the Patterson Archive and may be incomplete due to scrapbook cut-and-paste preservation.

PATTERSON SELECTED BIBLIOGRAPHY

Baker, Cindy L. "Life on the Elk Hills Oilfield." *The Taft Newsletter*, April 20, 2012, n.p.

Blodget, Hugh in Frank Latta. *Black Gold of the Joaquin*, op. cit.

Bridges, Ken. *History of Arkansas*. Online: www.southark.edu, n.d., n.p.

Curtis, Charles. "Trojan Spikers Loaded Despite Loss of Stars." *Los Angeles Times*, March 3, 1954, 25.

Dawn, Wenda. Cited in Baker, op.cit.

de la Vega, John. "Patterson's Mark in Shot Paces Preps." *Los Angeles Times*, May 25, 1952, n.p. [PA]

Del Mar, David B. "A Brief Early History of the Midway-Sunset Oil Field, 2001", Online: archives.datapages.com/data/pacific/data/093, n.p.

"Dixie Jo Ann Kenny to Wed Leon Patterson." *Taft Midway Driller*, May 27, 1953, 2.

Durslag, Melvin. Fragment of newspaper article [no title], *Los Angeles Examiner*, December 1954 [PA].

Eissinger, Michael. "Kern County: California's Deep South," paper presented at Critical Ethnic Studies and the Future of Genocide: Settler Colonialism/Heteropatriarchy/White Supremacy Conference. Riverside: University of California, March 2011. Online: www.academia.edu/1519415/Kern_County_Californias_Deep_South, n.p.

"Fellow Athletes Will Attend Patterson Rites." *The Bakersfield Californian*, Nov. 25, 1954. 35.

Ferguson, John L. in John Henry, op. cit.

"First Ribbon Won in County Competition -- Interest in Track Started at Early Age in School." *Taft Midway Driller*, November 26, 1954. n.p. [PA]

Fixico, Donald. "American Indians." Encyclopedia of Oklahoma History and Culture. Online: http://digital.library.okstate.edu/encyclopedia, n.d., n.p.

Gewecke, Cliff. "Trojan Track Athlete Patterson Dies." *Daily Trojan*, November 22, 1954, 1.

Gianopulos, Pete. "Remember When...?" *Taft Midway Driller*, Thursday May 2, 1996, n.p. (photocopy)

_____ (ed.). *The Taft Newsletter*. Multiple copies (1994-date).

Gregory, James N. American Exodus: *The Dust Bowl Migration and Okie Culture in California*. (New York: Oxford University Press, 1989).

Gustkey, Earl. "Hard Life and a Short Life." *Los Angeles Times*, Sports, April 30, 1991, C1, C8.

Haslam, Gerald, Stephen Johnson & Robert Dawson. *The Great Central Valley: California's Heartland*. Berkeley: University of California Press, 1993.

Haslam, Gerald. "Leon Patterson: A California Life of Promise." *The Bakersfield Californian*, July 14, 2012, online: bakersfieldcaliforian.com/opinion, n.p.

_____. "Leon Patterson's Short Season" in *The Other California: The Great Central Valley in Life and Letters* (Reno; University of Nevada Press, 1993), 175-180.

Heer, Clarence. *Income and Wages in the South*. (Chapel Hill: The University of North Carolina Press, 1950), 15.

Henning, Dr. Richard. TUHS Hall of Fame Induction Booklet, op. cit. [PA]

Henry, John. The Depression and Arkansas: Historians Shine Light On Dark Era. Online: http://jsor.org/discover, n.d., n.p.

"Historic Earthquakes/ Kern County, California/ 1952 07 21:14 UTC/ Magnitude 7.3." Online: http://earthquake.usgs.gov/earthquakes/states/events1952_07_21.php, n.p.

Hueler, Kenneth. "Life On An Oil Lease." *The Taft Newsletter*, November 10, 2012, 1-2.

Jagels, Stacey. "Interview with William Rintoul." *California Odyssey Project*. Bakersfield: California State University, 6/8/1981.

Johnson, Ben in John Henry, op. cit.

"Kern County Earthquake: Fiftieth Anniversary." Online: http://www.scec.org/education/020721kern.html, n.d., n.p.

Latta, Frank F. *Black Gold of the Joaquin*. Caldwell, ID: The Caxton Press, 1946.

"Leon Patterson Funeral Held Today in Taft — Large Crowd Pays Tribute to Great Athlete." *Taft Midway Driller*, November 26, 1954. n.p. [PA]

Ligget, Tom. "Patterson Sets New Shot, Discus Marks." *The Bakersfield Californian*, April 21, 1952. n.p. [PA]

"Local Track Pair Honored by Writers: Koch, Seaman Recognized for Top Week-end [sic] Marks." *Los Angeles Times*, n.d., n.p. [PA]

Masoumi, Mohammed Mikdi. "Influence of Oil Reservoir on Earthquake (IORE Theory)." *Research Journal of Environmental and Earth Sciences*, vol. 4 No. 9 (September 20, 2012). 818-822.

Mayer, Bill. "Sport Talk." *Lawrence Journal-World* December 7, 1954, n.p. [PA]

Mullins, William H. "Okie Migrations." *Encyclopedia of Oklahoma History and Culture*, 9, Oklahoma Historical Society, Online: http//digital,library.okstate.edu/encyclopedia/entries/O/OK008.html, n.d., n.p.

Murray, Gail S. "Forty Years Ago: The Great Depression Comes to Arkansas." *Arkansas Historical Quarterly* vol. 29, no. 4 (Winter, 1970), 291-312

Murray, Jim. "The Most Unwelcome Spectator." *Los Angeles Times*, Tuesday March 13, 1990, ports Section page 1, col. 2

Murray, Jim. "RE: LEON PATTERSON," unpublished, unedited manuscript for *Sports Illustrated*, dated Nov. 2, 1954 [PA]

Murray, Jim [Inferred byline]. "To an athlete," *Sports Illustrated*, December 6, 1954, 23-24.

Nezat, Dixie. Untitled, unpublished, handwritten memoir. Patterson Archive.

Nickell, Jeff. "Rising Above Dust Bowl Discrimination." *Bakersfield Life*, June 20113, 104-105.

"Patterson Succumbs in Southland — Bright's Disease Snuffs Out Life of Great Athlete." *The Bakersfield Californian*, November 22, 1954. n.p. [PA]

Rintoul, William. *Oildorado: Boom Times on the Westside*. Fresno: Valley Publishers, 1978.

_____. *Spudding In: Recollections of Pioneer Days in the California Oil Fields*. San Francisco: California Historical Society, 1976.

Russell, David Allen. "A Short Life." *A Writer's Soul*. October 23, 2006, 1-2.

Sooter, Rudy & Doy O'Dell. "Dear Okie" [song lyric]. c 1948.

Stein, Walter. *California and the Dust Bowl Migration*. (Westport, Connecticut: Greenwood Press, Inc., 1973)

Steinbeck, John. *The Grapes of Wrath*. New York: Viking Press, 1989

Taft Union High School Hall of Fame Induction [booklet]. Taft, CA: TUHS, April 30, 2011.

"The Second Great Migration." Online: www.inmotioname.org/print. cfm?migration+9&topic, n.d., n.p.

Sutton, Jerry. "Record Put Felt Bad — Slid Off Hand — Patterson." *Los Angeles Examiner*. May 25, 1952, Sec. 1, Part C.

Tinkham, Harley. "Trojan Discus Star in Battle to Save Sight, Discus Ace Victim of Tragedy." *Los Angeles Mirror* n.d., n.p. [PA]

"Trojan Discus Thrower Leon Patterson Dies." *Los Angeles Times*. November 22, 1954, C1.

"Trojan Track Athlete Leon Patterson Dies." *Daily Trojan*. Nov. 22, 1954, 1.

Weidman, Dr. Hazel M. Hitson in *TUHS Hall of Fame Induction booklet*, op. cit.

Windshuttle, Keith. "Steinbeck's Myth of the Okies (Another archetypical liberal myth debunked)," *The New Criterion*, June 2002, Online: www. newcriterion.com/articles.cfm/steinbeck-windshuttle-1941, n.p.

Wright, Bill, and Howard Herz. "Patterson Put Sets US Mark. *Los Angeles Examiner*, May 25, 1952, Sec. 1, Part C [PA]

INDEX

A

Albans, Bill, 51
Alcohol abuse, 9, 17, 20, 22, 33, 44, 68, 119, 126
Amick, Ron, 74
Arkansas, 3, 6, 8
Arkies, 6, 8, 18, 63
Arnett, Jon, 79, 91, 108

B

Bakersfield
    Committee of Sixty, 17
Bank, Dick, 89, 91, 93, 95, 113, 124, 127, 130, 131
Basham, Garland, 130
Bates, Phil, 130
Berryhill, Bruce, 33
Blodget, Hugh, 13
Bob Elias Sports Hall of Fame, 132
Boswell, Bill, 94, 101, 123, 126, 128, 130
Bridges, Ken, 7
Bright's disease, 4, 69, 70, 73, 113
Bugbee, Howard, 108
Bunche, Dr. Ralph, 55
Butcher, Mike, 58

C

California
    Agribusiness, 10
    Agriculture, 6, 119
    Anti-migrant, 17
    Migration, 8
    Poverty, 3, 119
    Public education, 24
    San Joaquin Valley, 9, 31
    Social class, 31
Campbell, Milt, 85
Chamber, Dwight, 91
Collins, Dr. John, 35
Collins, Tom, 7
Crawford, Reverend J. Alvin, 130
Crites, Arthur S., 17
Crunk, Joe, 130
Cutland, Dennis, 26, 81

D

Daily Trojan, 129
Dalton, Elvie, 26, 56, 83, 98, 130
Dawn, Wenda, 16
de la Vega, John, 2, 82
Decker, Jim, 79, 91
Derby Acres, 15, 19, 20, 22, 44
Dillon, Jim, 113

Donnell, Cork, 56
Dripping, 41
Duncan, Jim, 38
Durslag, Melvin, 94
Dust Bowl, The, 6, 8
Dykes, Dr. Dick, 130
Dykes, Patricia, 112
Dykes, Richelle, 99
Dykes, Suzanne, 99

E

Eissinger, Michael, 15
Ellingson, Darryl, 79
Erickson, John, 132
Evans, Lee, 23

F

Farm Security Administration, 18
Ferguson, John L., 7
Findley, Jack, 108
Flood, William, 130
Foutch, Pat, 50
Freeman, Bruce, 29, 37, 38
Freeman, Ralph "Dad", 42
Fresno, 71

G

Garcia, Mike, 23
Garrett, Mike, 49
Garrison, Jeanine, 99
General Petroleum Camp, 16
Gianopulos, Pete, 19, 80, 141
Gifford, Frank, 23

Goldman, Dr. Leon, 70
Gordien, Fortune, 52, 79, 96, 110, 114
Graffio, Joe, 108
Grapes of Wrath, The, 3, 17, 117
Great Central Valley, 10
Westside, 13
Great Depression, The, 5, 8, 27, 28, 93
Green, Gary, 26, 56, 83, 98, 130
Gregory, James, 8, 32, 34, 35, 62
Griffith, Dr. George C., 124
Gustkey, Earl, 3, 9, 38, 41, 68, 124, 129, 132, 134, 138, 139

H

Hanna, Dr. Charles, 26, 29, 42, 53, 78
Harrell, Alfred, 17
Harrelson, J.B. "Cap", 80
Hastings, Russell Eugene, 133
Hearndon, Hugh, 50
Henning, Dr. Richard "Dick", 16, 24, 39, 42, 63, 73, 83, 88
Herman, Ray, 26, 56, 78, 89, 91
Hillis, John, 7
Hoffman, Bob, 56
Hollingsworth, David, 65, 90
Hooper, Darrow, 1
Howard, Jack, 48

I

Iness, Sim, 23, 87, 93, 96, 104, 110, 127, 130, 134, 137

J

Jamerson, Pat, 32
James, Glenn "Tex", 29, 37
Johnson, Ben, 6
Johnson, Dean, 28
Johnson, Eugene, 130
Johnson, Jimmy, 23
Johnson, Rafer, 23, 137
Johnston, Eugene, 130
Jones, Larry Dean, 133
Jones, Riley, 58, 133

K

Kenney, Dixie, 4, 20, 32, See Patterson, Dixie
    Academics, 42, 72
    Awards, 42, 59, 72
    Married - Leon Patterson, 98
    Outstanding Female Athelete, 25
    Parents, 67
    Sports, 39, 42, 77, 96
    Work, 67
Kenney, Maurice, 41, 86, 133
Kenney, Minnie, 42, 133
Kenney, Patricia, 41
    aka - Mrs. Dick Dykes, 99
Kent, Emory, 83
Kern County, 17, 27
King, Leamon, 23, 137
Knick, Bill, 81
Koch, Des, 79, 96, 111, 113, 134
Kooken, Charlie, 32
Korean War, 76, 97

Krunk, Joseph, 130
Ku Klux Klan, 15

L

Larrabee, Mike, 108
Larsen, Jack, 91, 113, 122, 127, 128, 130, 131
Lea, Jim, 108
LeBaron, Eddie, 23
Ledesma, Fernando, 91
Levack, Wally, 108
Liggett, Tom, 80
Los Angeles Times, 38, 132, 138

M

Mathias, Bob, 23, 27, 51, 72, 85, 87, 134, 137
Mathias, Jim, 72, 94
Mayer, Bill, 3
McCabe, Gail, 99
McCabe, Neal, 77
McKee, Walter, 62
McManus, Thomas, 17
McNeish, Bob, 124
Midway Driller, 48, 80, 96, 97, 98
Midway-Sunset oilfield, 14
Migrants, 9, 12, 18, 31, 33, 35
    Dialects, 32
    Jobs, 17
Morris, Lige, 37
Morris, Ron, 91, 109, 128, 129
Mortensen, Jess, 78, 111, 129, 130, 134
Mulford, Gary, 81

Mullen, Vern "Moon", 28
Mullins, William H., 9
Murray, Jim, 19, 122, 129, 132

N

National AAU Championships, 114
National Collegiate Athletic Association Championships, 112
Nestell, Bud, 66
Newly, Bailey, 75
Nezat, Dixie. See Patterson, Dixie
    Death, 133, 134
    Interview, 9, 138
Nezat, Jerry Wayne, 133
Nezat, Mara Angela, 133
Nickell, Jeff, 31
Nieder, Bill, 1-4, 79, 81, 85

O

O'Brien, Dolores, 34, 68, 69, 81, 113, 134, 138
O'Brien, Parry, 48, 92, 96, 110, 130
O'Brien, Tom, 29, 34, 42, 47, 48, 49, 58, 68, 70, 71, 77, 80, 98, 130, 131, 132, 134, 137
Ogilvie, Gary, 48, 100
Okies, 6, 8, 18, 31

P

Patterson III, Orel Leon, 133
Patterson, Calvin, 3, 5, 24, 28, 33, 134
Patterson, Dixie
    Maiden name. See Kenney, Dixie
    Married - Jerry Wayne Nezat, 133
    Married - Riley Jones, 133
    Memoir, 135
    Pregnancy, 106, 112
    Work, 100, 101, 104, 116
Patterson, George, 3, 5, 8, 9, 12, 17, 19, 24, 28, 33, 55, 70, 71, 126, 128, 131
Patterson, Jr., Orel Leon (Lee), 44, 133, 138
    Birth, 112
Patterson, Kenney Ernest, 133
Patterson, Leon, 124
    Academics, 12, 20, 23, 32, 34, 79, 84, 95
    All-American, 114
    Ambitions, 33, 111
    Awards, 38, 50, 56, 59, 60, 61, 81
    Birth name, 5
    Death, 128
    Early life, 5
    First track meet, 24
    Funeral, 130
    Health, 69, 76, 93, 104, 108, 114, 120, 124
    Influences, 33, 49, 50, 68, 93
    Nicknames, 28
    Parents, 9, 44, 126, 131
    Record, 80, 82
    Sports, 2, 24, 35, 37, 47, 49, 57, 78
    Surrogate parents, 87, 134

Taft Union High School
    Football, 29
Taft Union High School Hall of
    Fame, 132
    University of Southern
        California, 79, 89
    Wedding, 98
    Work, 3, 9, 21, 38, 43, 69, 74, 90,
        99, 115
Patterson, Lillie, 5, 8, 9, 19, 43, 96,
    133, 134
Patterson, Marvin, 5, 7, 9, 15, 17, 19,
    24, 133, 134
Peahl, Lawrence "Larry", 48, 59, 129
Price, Bob, 139
Pryor, John, 50

R

Reedy, Monty, 28, 70, 134, 137
Richards, Rev. Bob, 72
Richter, Les, 23
Rintoul, William, 14, 15, 16, 29
Robinson, Ancel, 137
Russell, Richard, 49

S

Sceales, Dewey, 50
Schmitt, Archie, 49
Scruggs, Otey, 51, 72
Seamon, Bob, 23
Seaver, Tom, 23
Selective Service Act, The, 27
Sewell, Ed, 65
Shelton, Ernie, 108
Shelton, Lynne O'Brien, 34, 131
Shugart, Hillman "Shug", 29
Simmons, Floyd, 51, 72
Smith, Paul, 28
Smith, Tommie, 23
Snyder, Dick, 50
Snyder, Fred, 71
Soule, Frederick, 7
Sports Illustrated, 132
Spurrier, Lon, 23, 137
Standard Camp, 16
Stark, Milt, 36, 37
Stein, Walter, 18, 34
Steineger, Mrs., 39
Stiles, Maxwell, 130
Stineberg, Dale, 71
Switzler, Ted, 78, 81

T

Taft, 3, 10, 11, 13, 62, 129
    Oil Industry, 14
    Racial population, 30, 111
    Taft Union High School, 1, 23, 26
        Hall of Fame, 132
Thompson, Wilbur "Moose", 80
Tinkham, Harley, 124
Track & Field News, 61
Tupman Camp, 16

U

University of Southern California,
    78, 89
    Community, 129
    Leon Patterson Award, 132

Urquhart, Elvin, 30, 38, 40, 47, 52-54, 64, 65, 72, 81, 83, 104, 130, 132, 134

V

Vick, Don, 82
Voorhees, Les, 47, 50, 65
Vukovich, Billy, 23

W

Walrath, Sudie, 39
Warren, Earl, 111
Weidman, Dr. Hazel Hitson, 10, 16, 22, 24
Werdel, Charles (Chuck), 58, 134
West Coast Relays, 81
Wetter, Clyde, 60
Wilger, Rod, 91, 108
Windschuttle, Keith, 8
Wooliver, Jerry, 81
World War II, 8, 26, 27
Wright, Willard, 108

Y

Young, Patrick, 49

Z

Zumbro, Don, 26, 32, 37, 47, 78, 83